A BIT
of a
LAUGH

*A Real-Life Journey Into the World
of Stand-Up Comedy*

BEN TIFFEN

First published in Australia by Aurora House
www.aurorahouse.com.au

This edition published 2022
Copyright © Ben Tiffen 2022

Cover design: Donika Mishineva | www.artofdonika.com
Typesetting and e-book design: Amit Dey

The right of Ben Tiffen to be identified as Author of the Work has been asserted in accordance with the Copyright, Designs and Patents Act 1988.

ISBN number: 978-1-922697-30-1 (Paperback)

All rights reserved. No part of this publication may be reproduced, stored in a retrieval system, or transmitted, in any form or by any means without the prior written permission of the publisher, nor be otherwise circulated in any form of binding or cover other than that in which it is published and without a similar condition being imposed on the subsequent purchaser.

 A catalogue record for this book is available from the National Library of Australia

Distributed by: Ingram Content: www.ingramcontent.com
Australia: phone +613 9765 4800 |
email lsiaustralia@ingramcontent.com
Milton Keynes UK: phone +44 (0)845 121 4567 |
email enquiries@ingramcontent.com
La Vergne, TN USA: phone +1 800 509 4156 |
email inquiry@lightningsource.com

ACKNOWLEDGEMENTS

This is the story of somebody who has always been a massive admirer of comedians and their art, and on the cusp of his fortieth birthday decided to give stand-up comedy a go. Most of all, it's a story about indulging in your passions and trying something new, as you never know the extraordinary experiences it can lead to or the amazing people you can meet.

Throughout this journey I've met many wonderful, wise and most of all hilarious people. You will read about most of them here. But I would like to begin by acknowledging a small handful, including Kieran Butler, Evan Hocking, Mimi Shaheen, Stephen Rosenfeld, Adam Jacobs and Paul Blackburn. Thank you for the opportunities, mentorship, inspiration, friendship and drink cards.

And a heartfelt thanks to Sarah, as without you this story might have finished around Chapter Eight. Your companionship and support have always been highly valued, likewise your endurance of many, many hours of amateur comedy. That is devotion of the highest order.

Finally, my biggest thank you is for Matthew, who I describe in Chapter Two as my favourite travelling companion. That is true on so many levels. You inspire me most of all.

CONTENTS

Stepping up	1
Free comedy	11
Gold dust	21
Through the ages	29
Fifteen seconds	47
The next steps	59
The Golden State	71
Business time	87
Love and LOLs	101
The Lounge	117
Turbo charged	129
Raw	143
Da Bomb	157
Big Apple	165
Gotham	181
Fringe	199
Full circle	217
The Big Gig	237
About the Author	255

> *"Life is supposed to be fun, it's not a job or an occupation. We're here only once and we should have a bit of a laugh."*
>
> **Billy Connolly**

1
STEPPING UP

Jerry Seinfeld, one of my favourite comedians, has a famous routine in which he notes that public speaking is the average person's greatest fear. Death is number two.

Every word of that routine was making perfect sense to me as I sat waiting to be announced on stage. It was a Wednesday night in August 2013, and at age thirty-nine I was making my debut as a stand-up comedian in a pub in the Melbourne suburb of Richmond. Even though I was accustomed to speaking to audiences every day in my job as a secondary teacher, death at this moment was an alternative I would have at least considered. I felt sick. What the hell had I been thinking?

The MC, an impressive young comic named Taco, was warming up the crowd after the interval. I was the first act of the second bracket, and as Taco began a rather long story (I have no memory of anything he actually spoke about) I sat at a table about halfway back in the venue with my stomach in my mouth and my eyes fixed firmly on the floor. His story felt like it was going for *hours*. I glanced up again at the crowd around me, which seemed much larger than the thirty or so people in the room. None of them knew I was the next act – such is the nature of open mic nights – and I would have seriously considered going to the bathroom and escaping through a window if I hadn't invited family and friends to witness my first 'gig'.

As Taco's stories continued, the wait became excruciating and a strange thing happened – I mentally left the room. I can clearly remember having one of those weird out-of-body moments when you feel as though you're not really where you are. It was a classic head in the sand reaction to the fact that I was probably about to humiliate myself in public. I pictured a happy place, and the motivational speaker who had recently inspired me to step out of my comfort zone – whose head I would now happily flush in the toilet.

I was jerked back to reality by the sound of my own name.

'... And now please welcome to the stage our next act – give it up for Ben Tiffen!'

To expectant applause I rose and stepped up to the stage, shook hands with Taco, and fumbled the microphone from its stand. Looking at the audience, I could make out only shapes through the glaring stage lights. I tried hard to remember my opening line, the one I'd been practising all week.

Then, I spoke...

Three months earlier, I was getting a haircut. I had a short back and sides and an epiphany. It was the first of two moments that convinced me I should give stand-up comedy a go.

Rose had been cutting my hair for fifteen years, and reminded me that I'd been thinking about trying stand-up for quite some time.

'You're not getting any younger,' she noted as she shaved my ears. 'When are you going to just step up and do it?'

'I will, Rose, one day soon.'

'Ha, *one day!* How often does *one day* ever really come?'

She might have had a point. Was I becoming one of those people who say they're going to do stuff but never get around to doing it? It's easy to be one of those people, you can do so without lifting a finger.

'Ok, maybe on the summer holidays. I'm just so busy at the moment.'

'But you're always busy. If it's something you really want to do, why wait? When do you turn forty?'

My birthday was at the end of the year, but so far I hadn't given much thought to turning forty. Too much is made of numbers ending in zero, I believe. But maybe Rose was right. I *was* always busy. And perhaps when we're busy we can miss out on achieving life goals by not making enough time for them.

I've always been a massive fan of comedy. As a kid I loved staying up late to watch *The Big Gig*, a multi-stage live show on the ABC which featured many of Australia's best comics of the 1980s. Despite living just down the road from the ABC studios in Elsternwick, we couldn't get good reception on Channel Two unless someone physically held the TV antenna; as soon as you'd let go, host Wendy Harmer's face would look like an alien from *Dr Who*. I would hold the antenna for a whole hour – alternating arms as they grew tired – in order to catch every word, every nuance of language these talented artists would deliver.

From an early age I studied drama on Saturday mornings in a junior program at the National Theatre in St Kilda. I loved drama – particularly its comedic element. We'd often create funny skits or compete in theatre sports, similar to the modern show *Whose Line is it Anyway?* At school I ripped it up in drama class, winning the Year Eight subject award – a small, green plastic frog from my favourite teacher Mr Harmon, who made a speech about me at assembly that I'll never forget. No other trophy has survived all these years, but 'The Kermit' still sits proudly on my desk. I attribute drama to helping build my confidence as a young person, and I'm eternally grateful to my parents, Ron and Kama Tiffen, for encouraging me to pursue it. Sadly, I fell out of love with drama once my teenage years set in and other interests took over. I wish I'd stuck with it for longer.

By my thirties, I began to feel a pull back to the stage. I'd looked into drama classes for adults but nothing seemed to resemble what I'd enjoyed in the past, and I wasn't really up for the commitment of a theatre group. By now my lifelong love of stand-up comedy was beginning to look appealing as more than just something to watch. It was the perfect chance to get back on a stage. As an artform, stand-up is convenient. It neatly packages both writing and performing, and requires no expensive equipment. All I had to do was stand up and talk. Just talk. *How hard could it be?*

'You know what, Rose? I think you're right. I need to give comedy a go. Perhaps I do need to try it before I turn forty. I should have got into it years ago.'

'That's more like it,' she said. 'The sooner the better. Just make sure you let me know when you're on so I can come and throw tomatoes at you.'

I've often found haircuts to be a rather self-reflective experience. Rose could make them feel like a good therapy session – she always saw things clearly. Haircuts are also the only time most people will spend half an hour staring at themselves in a mirror. It was in one of those moments that I realised I should have reconnected with myself as a performer years ago. I'd always been meaning to but had let way too much time slip past. Maybe procrastination is a lot like other bad habits; the first step is acknowledging that you have a problem in the first place.

At roughly the same time, a motivational speaker came to our school. I teach mostly senior English and the VCAL (Victorian Certificate of Applied Learning) program, which is an alternative course for students interested in any of the great career pathways that don't involve going to university. I love my job, and particularly enjoy working with this age group – young people on the verge of adulthood finding their feet in the world. At the time, I worked at a large school in Melbourne's south-east. We'd had unmemorable motivational speakers in the past, but when Declan – a young bloke with a good energy about him – introduced himself as someone from the Reach program, I was instantly intrigued. I knew Reach to have done inspiring work with young people impacted by adversity. Its co-founder, AFL football legend Jim Stynes, had passed away from cancer the previous year. I was surprised to learn he'd started this program well *before* his diagnosis. I'd always presumed it to be something he did as a celebrity to help others going through a similar ordeal, but Stynes had started Reach years earlier purely out of the goodness of his Irish heart. Declan was quite emotional as he recounted how much Stynes had helped him overcome his own mental health issues.

Declan began with some jokes about teachers (the standard way for school speakers to build rapport) and then placed a chair in front of the group of about a hundred Year Twelve students and announced that, one by one, every student in the room was going to stand on the chair and sing for thirty seconds. No exceptions. And there were rules; it had to be a proper song, no nursery rhymes, footy songs or TV themes – just a fair dinkum song for at least thirty seconds. He asked for a volunteer to go first.

Nobody moved.

Silence engulfed the room as he waited. All eyes went straight to the floor. Undeterred, Declan simply waited in silence. He took a seat and continued waiting.

Minutes dragged past as he continued to wait.

It was the most awkward silence imaginable and I wondered if it was going to last the whole two hours until recess. It would have seemed funny to students except by now they were way too scared to laugh, or even make eye contact with each other, as any slight movement would draw attention to them. Even I stared at the floor and inwardly scrambled to think of a song in case he chose a teacher to get up as an ice-breaker. The wait extended to a ridiculous point until Jarrod, a tall boy with shaggy hair, remarkably stepped up and stood on the chair. The whole room breathed a sigh of relief. Jarrod tentatively sang a verse and chorus of Ed Sheeran's *The A-Team* and received tumultuous applause. I remember thinking at the time it was one of the bravest acts I'd seen.

With the tension slightly relieved, a few other students stepped up to sing a few lines, gradually relaxing into the experience and having some fun with it. Of course, Declan did not really expect everybody to get up, and announced that it had been an exercise in stepping out of your 'comfort zone'.

Declan then drew a large circle that took up a whole whiteboard and asked students to consider their comfort zone when they were five years old. Was it bigger or smaller than it is now? In other words, would they have found it easier to sing in front of peers when they were in Prep or in Year Twelve? Of course, the answer was the former. Declan drew a much smaller circle inside the larger one to demonstrate the difference between typical comfort zones from Prep to Year Twelve, and asked students to consider why theirs may have shrunk so much over the years. Self-consciousness, fear of ridicule, pride and fear of failure were some responses. This began a very engaging discussion on the traps of living within a comfort zone and failure to challenge yourself to expand it. So many students were suddenly able to open up about their insecurities and fears, some quite publicly. They began to understand that what was holding them back at times was merely their self-doubt. There were genuine tears from students and staff alike, and to this day it is one of the most powerful lessons I've witnessed.

We've happily had the Reach program back for more and, from a personal perspective, it was a good kick in the bum. These seminars aren't aimed at teachers, but I was now even more determined to step up on the comedy stage. After seeing and hearing so many great examples of young people challenging themselves to bravely confront their anxieties, I really had no more excuses. If Jarrod could sing in front of his entire Year Twelve cohort, surely I could tell a few jokes to a room full of strangers.

I began researching comedy venues around Melbourne that very evening.

The audience at Station 59 in Richmond waited keenly for my opening line.

'So why do people say it's good luck when a bird shits on you?'

The words didn't come out quite as confidently as they had at home. My nerves were impossible to hide, and the crowd smelt my fear. Nervousness can be a set killer, as no matter how good material may be, it's never going to work if the audience is cringing for you. But it wouldn't have mattered anyway. I had a whole segment about bird shit.

'A bird shat on my head the other day,' I announced. 'But it was probably my fault, I shouldn't have asked her to sleep on the couch.'

Silence pounded in my ears. While I thought this joke was ok at the time, it lacked originality and I lacked confidence. I must admit it was an adaptation of a joke I'd heard before, which went along the lines of a bird shitting on a guy's car so he 'never asked her out again'. Even though I thought my version was an improvement, I learned immediately that you can't simply change the context of a joke to make it a new joke. Who would have ever thought that was ok? Comedy lesson number one.

'So I was in London last year,' I announced, knowing the rest of my routine was at least original, 'and an English bloke called me the C-word… convict.'

More silence. I honestly can't even remember what I said next. On some level I think I've blocked it out. There was a bit about the cricket, and general observations about the English, but even that didn't raise a single chuckle. I moved on to some jokes about Facebook, probably rather cliché I'm sure, and still got nothing. The small stage began to feel huge. I glanced at my friends Teddy, Andrew and Alison, who I'd been banking on for some fake laughs if nothing else, but they were just smiling in the way one might do when a preschooler tells a long story and you want to encourage them. As I thought of my next line, I could hear a conversation from the smoking area outside.

I pushed through to the end of my routine, feeling the stab of embarrassment but at the same time no pressure to get off the stage. I was a first-time comic, like others I'd witnessed here, and while the crowd was not going to give me any undeserved laughs, at least I wasn't being disrespected. That's what I like about many open mic venues, you're allowed to suck. So I continued sucking to the very end. And, to be honest, I was still proud of myself as I thanked the crowd and shook hands with Taco on the way offstage.

'Was that your first time?' he asked delicately.

'Um... yes.'

'Well done, man. That was great.'

I sat down more relieved than I can remember, instantly realising this caper was far more difficult than I had imagined. I'd been terrible. Completely out of my depth. But still, I had to remember it had been a lifetime, in a way, since I'd performed on a stage, and it would naturally take a while to get over the nerves and feel comfortable again. So despite the embarrassing result, I actually went home feeling satisfied knowing I'd at least challenged myself to step out of my comfort zone, and in doing so fulfilled a lifelong ambition and done something most people would be too scared to attempt. I'd just performed stand-up comedy. And while the journey to becoming any good at it was suddenly looking much longer than I'd anticipated, I vowed to not give up after one nervous debut. It felt good to break out of my comfort zone, and I wanted more.

My next goal in comedy was to hear a laugh.

2

FREE COMEDY

Station 59 accurately described itself as 'The little pub with a big heart'. Nestled between housing commission flats on one side of Church Street and some of Melbourne's most expensive real estate on the other, it had a homely feel that seemed to have survived the changing landscape of Richmond. I learned that my father's side of the family used to drop in here for a beer when it went by a different name many years earlier. Its decor presently had a fire brigade theme as it was next to Richmond Fire Station. Among the current decoration was an authentic bronze pole from which a mannequin fireman descended, rushing bravely towards a danger from which most would run.

I'd found Station 59 through a basic Google search for open mic comedy venues. Embarking into comedy from scratch, I had no idea where to begin. Despite being a great fan of stand-up, I'd had very little exposure to the amateur scene. Like most people, I associated comedy only with the big names of the industry, the polished professionals, without really considering where they'd started. But, as I was soon to discover, the amateur comedy circuit in Melbourne is huge and vibrant. And very, very diverse.

The term 'open mic' is at times misunderstood. To outsiders it may sound as though anyone who is out for a night can walk up to a microphone and say whatever they like, however that is certainly not the case. I've even heard open mic likened to karaoke – a comparison considered an insult by those on the circuit. Open mic comedians normally toil long and hard to prepare material, and to get a spot can take weeks. Karaoke is drunk people singing *Khe Sahn*.

Free Comedy 59, the open mic comedy show running every Wednesday, defined itself by the maxim of 'No cliques. No fear. No favour'. It was a quality I would later learn to set it above many others. It was run by Kieran Butler – a highly experienced comedian and all-round top bloke. I recognised some of his great work, including musical comedy, from sports radio station SEN. Kieran offered a five to seven minute spot to anyone who asked. However, it was good form – in fact, an unwritten law in the open mic scene – to support the room by first attending as an audience member and getting to know the hosts. I selected Station 59 as my first venture and turned up in mid-2013 to enjoy my first true night of open mic comedy. My induction into a thriving world that until now I had barely known existed.

And for this journey I took my favourite travelling companion of all: my son Matthew. I became a proud dad at a young age, and Matthew was now old enough to join me in pubs. Matthew grew up in a good home with his mother on the Mornington Peninsula and I'm blessed to have always maintained a close relationship with him. Now that he was older and less frequently sleeping over on weekends, it was important to find other ways to spend time together. Comedy became a wonderful experience to share, and from early on Matt and I became astute critics. We've always shared a similar sense of humour. When going to movies we will normally select a good comedy with clever writing over a banal action film, and we had enjoyed going to several comedy festival shows in recent years. Matt has always been very creative. He has a passion for writing song lyrics and is currently emerging as a talented rap artist, having already produced many of his own tracks.

Another strong passion we've shared is for chicken parmigiana. We have long enjoyed evaluating our parmas by a range of criteria, including presentation. For example, if the parma is placed on top of the chips, turning them soggy from tomato paste, it will score lowly. Fortunately, on our first night at Station 59 the meals met our standards, so Wednesdays became a regular catch up for father and son for a good while. It's frightening to consider how different my journey might have been if we'd received a microwaved chicken schnitzel left over from the night before.

I can't quite remember most of the acts from our first open mic experience, but I do remember one thing – some of them didn't get many laughs. That's what first strikes you about amateur comedy. When watching the big festival galas on TV we see the best five minutes of the best performers in the country. When sitting in a Richmond pub on a Wednesday night we see where they started and where a lot of others gave up. I certainly don't mean that in a derogatory way, as without these venues there would be no festival galas. Those who traverse these stages are some of the bravest comics going around, and it's people like Kieran who provide the foundation for Melbourne's internationally renowned comedy scene. But if you're looking for a big night of laughs, it's probably important to remember why open mic comedy is almost always free. Some nights can be side-splitting, but others can be long, gruelling affairs. It's very hit-and-miss.

During this period we enjoyed watching many experienced comedians over many uproarious nights at Station 59, and Wednesday soon became my favourite night of the week. We also saw many others at various levels of learning the craft, and it became increasingly clear how much trial and error it can take. Like any new skill worth learning, the amount of practice, hard work and experimentation that can go into stand-up is invisible to those who are only exposed to the elite. In comedy, this can be especially deceptive; with no props or instruments to master, it probably seems like anyone who is naturally funny could be good at it straight away. But I soon came to understand that it doesn't work like that. Despite popular belief, there are very few natural stand-up comedians. Some will admit to being class clowns, while others will say they were, like me, more on the introverted side (which makes sense as introverts are more observational), however all will tell you they had to work hard at it. Some can be very funny in their first gig, but to be consistently funny takes a lot of experience with a wide variety of audiences and venues. It is only through devotion and perseverance that comedians progress, and this, in part, was what we were watching. Over the next few weeks, Matt and I were to observe many of the same performers returning to ply their craft. Some seemed to do it just for fun, while others appeared more focused on continually advancing.

It also became clear that, just like any other artform, comedy has a myriad of styles and genres, and at open mic nights you never know what to expect. There might be a stoner doing drug jokes, which can feel like it's taking forever, then a young feminist, then an ethnic satirist, and then a fortyish first-timer like me. Normally it's fun to have that element of surprise, but also, like any other artform, comedy can be extremely subjective. Humour is a quality that distinguishes us as individuals, which is a great thing overall, but a frightening prospect when attempting to make a room full of people laugh. I've actually met people who can't stand Billy Connolly, Jerry Seinfeld or Dave Hughes. If those people were in my audience, what chance did I have of winning them over? At open mic venues, however, many comics don't seem to care too much about wide appeal. They just take pleasure in stepping up, having a voice and appealing to at least a niche audience. That is one of the great values of amateur comedy communities such as this one, but for the audience it's important to know that anything can go at open mic. I've seen people laughing heartily at one act then walking out during the next. Some material can go to very dark places. And while dark material can be confronting and occasionally hard to laugh at, in some ways it is this free artistic expression that I was finding to be the strength of open mic comedy. This was the uncensored comedy scene. A comedy 'democracy', as Kieran has proudly described it. Some comedians could be perversely funny, and others would just find value in being heard. I was soon to glean that *'Free Comedy'* was not just a reference to price.

This was, of course, completely new to Matt and me, but as we observed more comedians on this circuit we began to appreciate their work with more insight. Some were hilarious and overall we found great value in committing our Wednesday nights to Station 59. Many times we'd be watching through tears of laughter and I wondered why it had taken me so long to discover this wonderful scene. Also in this time, we frequented *Five Boroughs Comedy* in an upstairs bar in the city, a hidden gem of a room that often featured the biggest names in Australian comedy trialling new material. In a short period we saw Mick Molloy, Tony Martin, Ronny Chieng, Jeff Green, Adam Rozenbachs, Celia Pacquola and Joel Creasy. It offered a great chance to see the elite professionals up close. But to be honest, it was Station 59 with its raw unpredictability that grew on me the most. Matt and I would analyse the best acts in depth as I drove him home each week. By now he lived in Essendon, and I really came to value these reflective late night drives.

'What did you think of the Harold Holt guy?' I once asked in response to one of our favourites, Garry Johal, who questions how Australia can simply lose a Prime Minister for swimming out too far.

'He's your Prime Minister – he's not a puppy!'

Matt and I agreed that Johal had an insightful perspective as a young comedian who was born and raised in Singapore, and that cultural observations from the outside can work well at all levels of comedy.

'What about Sofie's dilemma?' This was in response to the charismatic regular Sofie Prints, who'd been disappointed that none of her friends seemed to care when she had texted them that she was locked out of her house. 'But then I checked my sent box and I'd written *I've licked myself out...* [pause for a big laugh] No response *is* the correct response.' We discussed how the concept of placing yourself in a dilemma was an age-old form of humour, and pondered why, as a human race, we never get sick of it.

'I liked the *Ghost* guy, he's really genuine,' I said, and Matt concurred, in response to a young man with dark curly hair and a ragged leather jacket. He would begin by saying 'Do you think you've seen me before? Well, who's seen the movie *Ghost* with Patrick Swayze?' A pause would be followed by a guttural 'Get off my train!' His name was Tony Magnusson, and a sneaky Google search revealed that he does, indeed, bear a slight resemblance to the actor who plays the bum ghost living in the subway, and Tony used this brilliantly to his advantage.

As much fun as we were having, the overarching purpose of our venture into the world of comedy was ever present and Matt was growing increasingly keen for my debut performance. I'd been enjoying our regular catch ups, and perhaps I'd been stalling somewhat, but the time had come for me to step up. It was time to drag myself out of my comfort zone. So I asked Kieran for a spot and he slotted me in for the following week. Unfortunately, he wasn't going to be there himself as he was off to perform at the Edinburgh Comedy Festival, but there would be other comics filling in as MC while he was away. Suddenly it all became very real. Despite feeling reasonably confident, the nerves appeared immediately and I reminded myself of the same things I tell my students every time they get nervous before a class presentation – 'You're only nervous because you care about doing a good job' and 'Imagine how proud you will feel when it's over'. I was about to find out whether my own advice was any bloody good.

And I was particularly looking forward to the in-depth analysis Matt would provide on the way home from my first gig. By now we'd both become relative experts on good and bad open mic comedy, and it would be wonderful to get his insight into my performance and deconstruct it in depth as we do with so many others.

We were pretty silent until about the Bolte Bridge.

'Your act was... good,' he finally offered. 'For your first time, it was no worse than some other first time acts we've seen.'

'Aww, thanks mate,' I replied earnestly. I could tell he was feeling an odd combination of pride and sympathy. But there was no reason for him to feel sorry for me.

'I think some of your bits had potential,' Matt said, 'but I don't think the audience really related to some of your references, like the one about the London Tube – that would probably only be funny to someone like you who's been there.'

Matt was right. I was impressed with how perceptive he was becoming, and we spoke about other elements in detail – things I would have noticed in other people's comedy but overlooked in my own.

There were plenty of lessons to take out of this night, and while some of my material could still be rigorously panel beaten into much funnier shape, I'd feel better about scrapping it altogether and starting my writing process again. As we neared Matt's home he asked one final question, one that got me thinking more than any others. Among all of the analysis, I think we'd both suddenly remembered the real reason why I'd put myself through this whole ordeal.

'Did you enjoy it, Dad?'

It was not an easy question. Who would enjoy being embarrassed on stage? But still, I was leaning towards *yes*. Challenging yourself can feel very rewarding. I'm sure mountaineers don't always enjoy climbing mountains, but afterwards the feeling of conquering such a challenge would be euphoric. And while the 40cm raised stage was barely a mountain, I'd started a journey towards hopefully enjoying myself more every time I stepped onto it.

'You know what, in a way I actually did,' I replied.

I explained to Matt that as a kid I loved drama. I told him about my days at the National Theatre, where I'd felt truly creative and loved nothing more than to simply perform. To be introspective, my biggest motivation for becoming a comedian was probably to reconnect with that period of my life. Somehow, I'd lost my creative outlet along the way and I was enjoying finding it again. Matt was genuinely intrigued, and I reminded him of how important it is to always find time for your creativity to flourish. I'm glad he's never lost interest in his music.

Undeterred, I vowed to get back on the stage as soon as possible and to bring a much better act. Having experienced firsthand how deafening silence can be, I was determined to never 'hear' it again. I had to write better material as quickly as I could if I was going to accomplish my next goal in comedy. I was determined to get back on stage and finally hear laughter.

How hard could it be?

3
GOLD DUST

How to write good comedy material? At this stage it seemed I didn't know as much as I thought. It was time to start over, so I planned a writing weekend.

To get into a creative headspace I often enjoy going to my family's holiday house at Venus Bay, a sleepy coastal town in South Gippsland. I've always been an avid creative writer, and sometimes when I feel the urge to write I drive a couple of hours to where there is little noise but that of the waves breaking on the beach at the end of our street. Add to that the lack of phone and internet reception and for a writer it can be paradise. So with nothing but a couple of new A4 exercise books and a few beers, I made a solo journey to Venus Bay to spend a solid weekend writing comedy. I had another spot booked at Station 59 in a couple of weeks and I wanted this one to be much, much better. My goal was to write and practise at least five minutes of fresh, sharp material that would get some good, genuine laughs. Not just one laugh (though I'd take that as an improvement) but many.

It was a cold Friday night for spring, so I threw some redgum on the fireplace and set my creative writing playlist on shuffle – a mix ranging from U2 to Sting to just about anyone who has appeared on Smooth FM – and settled in for some solid writing. I poured a beer and opened a fresh exercise book, ironing out the fold with my hand. I've always loved the feel and smell of a new exercise book. It's a strange sensation I've enjoyed since childhood, in the same way an artist might feel inspired by a blank canvas. Unless I'm writing copious amounts, I still prefer an exercise book to a computer. I hoped that by Sunday it would be brimming with new ideas, jokes, routines and refinements just leaping off its pages, dying to be rehearsed. I picked up my favourite pen, an expensive one with a rubber cushion grip that I use only for special occasions, and then paused.

Now what?

I'd thought about everything so far, except what to actually write about.

I had a notebook of random ideas I'd been keeping for several years, anticipating a time I might actually use the material, but so far nothing was standing out. There were some observations about trams, and a bit about self-serve registers at supermarkets (I'm sorry Coles, but a bag is not an unexpected item in a bagging area), but nothing was leaping off the page as a big laugh. Then I noticed an idea I'd scribbled a few years ago about AIDS. Not the cheeriest of topics, however my experience with open mic comedy so far had told me that dark humour was not only acceptable, but probably my best chance to get a laugh at present. My idea – and note 'idea' in this sense does not mean joke or routine, but simply a random thought to hopefully be whittled into something humorous – regarded the commonly held belief that AIDS originated from someone having sex with a monkey.

When I'd first heard about AIDS it was not long after I'd first learned about sex, and one thing that had shocked me as a schoolboy in the 1980s was not just that AIDS was going to wipe out mankind (our generation was traumatised by an ad featuring the Grim Reaper knocking down people with a bowling ball; at one stage he even picked up a spare), but that it had started from somebody copulating with a primate. Even as a child I'd thought that point may have been somewhat glossed over. Now, years later, it seemed like a comedic gold nugget just waiting to be polished.

But how to make it funny? I was learning that a good premise doesn't always lead directly to good material. In fact, that is exactly where hard work comes into it. Making the leap from premise to belly laughs is where the experience, skill and labour kicks in, and I was still a long way from mastery.

'So… AIDS. They say it began by someone having sex with a monkey…'

Now what?

'At least he saved money on dinner and drinks.'

No, that's terrible.

'Must have been gaggin' for a root… maybe it was an Aussie Rugby League player stumblin' home from a Cape Town nightclub.'

Still terrible. Just abysmally atrocious! But maybe at least getting closer by introducing cultural references.

It was getting frustrating. I knew there was a big laugh in there somewhere but I couldn't find it. If the laugh was a gold nugget, I'd been panning for hours under the hot sun with no sign of it. *How hard could this be?* I'd come up with several ideas that sounded ok until I said them aloud and then questioned their originality – not that I'd heard them before, but if I was thinking of them so readily I felt there mustn't be anything too special about them. I'd observed from early on that predictability in comedy can be a set killer. If the audience gets to a punchline before the comedian they will moan, not laugh. This was doing my head in.

I began pacing the room. I poured another beer, feeling a bit heavy-hearted that so far I'd created more empty stubbies than funny jokes. From the stereo Bono was prattling on about some shit to do with world peace, and the fire was dying so I dumped more wood on it. It was beginning to feel like a wasted night and I was tempted to start rifling through my father's collection of DVDs that clearly lived up to the standard of holiday house movie selections. Elvis Presley in *G.I. Blues* seemed to be the newest release, and while I don't mind the music of Elvis, let's face it, his movie scripts were probably written in less time than it was taking me to write one joke about bestiality.

As a last-ditch effort, I looked back at my notebook for a fresh idea. There was an older scrawl I hadn't yet considered: 'Damien Leith – stalker'.

Damien Leith won the TV talent show *Australian Idol* in 2006. He was an Irishman who released a couple of singles before retreating back into relative obscurity. One of his singles was the acoustic ballad *22 Steps*, in which he romanticises the object of his affection by stating 'There's 22 steps to your door…'

Now, call me normal, but doesn't that sound just a bit creepy? In fact, it's up there with some of the creepiest songs of all time, including *Every Breath You Take* by The Police and *You're 16* by Ringo Starr ('You're 16, you're beautiful and you're mine,' crooned the thirty-four year old former Beatle). But for some reason, *22 Steps* became a brief hit in Australia and nobody saw anything weird about it.

Nobody, until now.

Too much time had passed to joke directly about Damien Leith. But the premise that appealed to me was the fine line between somebody being genuinely romantic and in love, and somebody who knows exactly how many steps are required to get to a front door. At what point does a romantic act become a disturbing one?

I knew that somewhere in there was a piece of comedic gold dust.

As I was introduced on stage at Station 59 for my second attempt at stand-up comedy, I was relieved there was a slightly smaller crowd. This reduced my nerves, which was ironic, as it also reduced my chance of getting good laughs. But for now I was happy. Matthew was by my side again, and remarkably, Teddy and Andrew had returned for more.

I energetically bounded on stage and greeted the room with a gushing proclamation that I was 'in love!' A group of women at one of the front tables gave an 'Aawww', and I was excited to have engaged them from the beginning.

'I actually fell in love with the girl next door. I know that's old fashioned, but it's been about six months now and I couldn't be happier.'

More delighted sounds from the women at this guy on stage who was clearly a top bloke.

'And do you know what I really enjoy about being in love? It's the little things. Like I really enjoy watching her drift off to sleep at night. I enjoy watching her wake up in the morning.'

'Aawww,' from the crowd.

'I enjoy watching her in the shower.'

A strategic pause for effect here as I escape lovingly into my mind.

'I don't actually know her name yet. But I do know there are fourteen steps to her bedroom window.'

The mood in the room suddenly turned cooler and I wondered if I'd overdone the creepiness. Of course, my son and mates gave me nothing, and I was almost about to resign myself to another silent set, when something extraordinary happened.

I heard a laugh.

It was a male laugh from the back of the room. And not just a snicker, it was a deep, genuine laugh from somebody who had clearly had their funny bone tickled. Nobody could have faked a laugh like that; nobody would have a reason to. For the first time ever, I felt like… dare I say it?

A comedian.

I don't know who the man was, but I now wish I could buy him a drink and let him know what a major impact he had on me at that moment. Former Australian Test cricket captain Steve Waugh describes in his autobiography the feeling of scoring his first run for his country as 'One run that nobody could ever take away from me'. I felt the same about my first laugh. Even if I never performed stand-up again, I'd made a stranger laugh. It was a moment of human connection. I'd earned that laugh and it could never be taken back. It's amazing how good that finally felt.

I continued into my bit about AIDS and was pleased to get a few more decent chuckles from most of the audience. It was nothing significant, and I never did that material again, but still I was ecstatic. I'd improved on my first gig and was finally hearing laughter. This comedy caper was quite a buzz!

I wanted more. In fact, I wanted much more.

And I wanted to learn as much about comedy as possible. In order to get good at any art form, I believe, it's important to understand it from its foundations. So I decided to do as much research as I could.

(Later I would come to realise that the stalker joke was way too dark to suit my persona. At this stage I was still not conscious enough of such things. However, my first laugh was still a proud moment and based not so much on the twist, but the fact that my character didn't seem to know his behaviour was wrong. There's a name for that – a 'comic flaw', where the audience has more awareness of a character fault than the storyteller does. These were all lessons to come; this exciting journey was just beginning...)

4

THROUGH THE AGES

Historians seem to agree that stand-up comedy originated from the vaudeville theatres of New York City that were popular around the turn of the twentieth century – fast-paced burlesque shows featuring dancing girls, striptease, contortionists, magicians, animal acts, music and slapstick humour. Crowds would be raucous and well refreshed with ale, often unwinding from a long working week. One theatre's advertisement in *The New York Herald* in 1893 declared cheerfully, 'To those whose minds are full of business cares and who do not feel up to following the dialogue and situations of a play which demands a certain amount of intellectual effort, vaudeville is a boon.' How could that not be fun?

Vaudeville humour originally involved pies in the face, crude innuendos, and impersonating people of other ethnic backgrounds. Basically, anything a Year Nine student would find amusing today would have a vaudeville audience in stitches. Evolving from this was a new style of performance – the comic monologue with no props or costumes – and to maintain the fast pace of the show, comics were required to develop tight, rapid-fire comedy with a new emphasis on set-up and punch. Vaudeville spoke to the common man, and comic monologues often featured topics such as financial struggles, nagging mothers-in-law and, much like today, laughing at those in authority. One of its earliest proponents was Groucho Marx, who pioneered the quick punchline artform. His snappy one-liners and double entendres inspired a whole era of comedians:

'I never forget a face, but in your case I'm happy to make an exception.'

'Marriage is an institution. But who wants to live in an institution?'

'Here's to our wives and girlfriends. May they never meet.'

Groucho emerged as the first prominent comedian to develop a distinctive stage persona. His exaggerated quirks included a cigar, stooped posture, and glasses and a moustache that resembled a modern-day novelty disguise. Eventually the vaudeville success of the Marx Brothers took them to Broadway to become the world's most famous comedic family – a claim they probably still have rights to more than a century after they first performed.

Bob Hope, one of comedy's biggest ever names, also got his start on the vaudeville circuit and was another master of set-up and punch one-liners. Perhaps his most iconic work was done with the military. He was the first stand-up comedian of note to entertain US troops abroad, first during World War II and then throughout the Korean, Vietnam and Persian Gulf wars. In total he made fifty-seven headline performances in some of the world's most dangerous war zones, an effort stretching from 1941–1991. Watching Hope perform to vast fields of soldiers in Vietnam is by far the most inspiring comedy footage I have seen (check it out on YouTube). Thousands of young but hardened faces laughing heartily together and forgetting, just briefly, that many of them may not make it home. In 1997, US

President Bill Clinton named Hope an 'Honorary Veteran', to which he replied, 'I've been given many awards in my lifetime, but this is the greatest honour I have ever received'. Hope died at the age of 100 in 2003. One cannot imagine a fuller life.

Throughout the 1960s to '70s, the traditional set-up and punch style began to make way for a more liberal and diverse range of styles, and individual persona became key. When a young Woody Allen first performed stand-up he was not always well received, or even understood, by his audiences. I originally knew Allen from *Take the Money and Run* – a film my younger sister Kathy and I watched so many times we could probably still recite it. Many years later, again thanks to the wonders of the internet, I enjoyed his early stand-up too. Allen spoke to his audience in a meek conversational style, seeming insecure and fretful and often searching for words. He came across as being so uneasy that most people were surprised to learn it was merely a well-rehearsed persona. Talk show host Dick Cavett was one of the first to publicly recognise Allen's brilliance by stating '...I resented the fact that the audience was too dumb to know what they were getting'. Allen's monologue style was also known for its brutally honest social and cultural commentary, with his signature pessimistic twist – 'Life is full of misery, loneliness, and suffering – and it's all over much too soon.'

Also known for his brusque social commentary was George Carlin, who became another favourite of mine, although not until after his death in 2008 did I pore over his footage. His persona evolved to be distinctively terse and disgruntled. Carlin's crassness was directly responsible for laws that remain in the US today, stipulating that language considered 'indecent' can only be aired after 10pm (although, by today's standards his language would barely stand out). He also became one of the most outspoken comic vilifiers of religion, and his funeral was marked by a picket-line from the maniacal Westboro Baptist Church.

By contrast, Steve Martin's nonsensical style saw him become a comedy rockstar. He ceased performing stand-up for the same reason the Beatles stopped playing live gigs. He would play stadiums – yes, *stadiums* – and be drowned out by the cheering crowds. Martin is the perfect example of a comedian who rose to the absolute top of his field through devotion and practice. From the age of ten he performed comedy magic multiple times a week, honing his craft throughout his entire youth and adolescence. You would swear he was just a naturally goofy guy, but it took him a lifetime to become that natural. And he was one of the first comics to be regarded as somewhat screwy, who veered away from the necessity of punchlines. TV talk show host Johnny Carson introduced him in 1973 with: 'If you haven't seen Steve's work before it's difficult to explain exactly what he does. It's usually something a little bit strange.' That was moments before Martin performed a live routine for an audience consisting purely of dogs.

While that might seem hard to top in terms of strangeness, Andy Kaufman's persona was sometimes so anxious and insecure that audiences were unsure whether they were supposed to laugh. On an early episode of *The David Letterman Show*, there is footage of the audience actually giving him money after a disturbing monologue about his unemployment that didn't contain a single joke. But therein lay the comedic value – this is a style known as anti-humour. Kaufman's most legendary comedy routine, where he lip-syncs the lyrics to the *Mighty Mouse* theme song, was aired on the very first episode of *Saturday Night Live* in 1975 and reprised many years later by Jim

Carrey in a biopic of Kaufman's life. Without saying a word, he puts on a record and mimes the line 'Here I come to save the day' with the fervour of a true cartoon superhero. For the rest of the song he just stands there nervously, riddled with anxiety and concentrating hard to come back in at the right time. His hands are twitching. His eyes are darting. His face is tense with concentration. He is a mess of insecurities. When he finally springs to life again as the self-assured Mighty Mouse, the audience is in raptures for him. Watching that footage can leave me crying with laughter, yet Kaufman doesn't say a single word.

The real boom for stand-up occurred in the late 1970s and '80s with the rise of comedy clubs across America. By the end of this period there were over 300 clubs showcasing comedians every night of the week, including now iconic venues such as The Improv and The Gotham Comedy Club in New York City, and The Comedy Store and Laugh Factory in Los Angeles. Comedy became big business, and it's no surprise that comedians of that era remain the most influential of all time.

Robin Williams was another idol of mine, though it wasn't until I was much older and past seeing him as the alien from *Mork and Mindy* that I appreciated his seemingly manic spontaneity and character voices. He was one of the world's best proponents of the 'act out' – mimicking conversations between two or more people – and his character humour translated perfectly from the comedy stage to the movie screen; he would step into eclectic roles, such as Mrs Doubtfire or a mad professor, barely changing stride.

Rather cheekily, in primary school some friends and I would listen to a cassette of Richard Pryor, sniggering at the rude bits and hastily turning it off when a teacher came by. I think it must have been his popular album *That Nigger's Crazy*, as I remember being alarmed by his frequent and bold use of a word we were told could never be spoken aloud. Comedy is often a vehicle for crashing headlong into social issues and Pryor, known for his close examination of racism, is widely regarded as the most empowering black comedian of all time. Modern day comedian Dave Chappelle said of Pryor's impact: 'You know those, like, evolution charts of man? He was the dude walking upright.' This was all unnoticed by me at that age; I just thought Pryor sounded funny and I laughed at his goofiness in *Superman 3*. From onerous beginnings (he was raised in a brothel by his alcoholic prostitute mother), he ascended to be ranked first in *Rolling Stone* magazine's recent list of the fifty greatest comedians of all time. First.

Steven Wright is a master of 'deadpan'. In a lethargic monotone, he will brood on philosophical issues: 'Change is inevitable... except from vending machines', or he will share more mundane experiences with a difference: 'I got a parking ticket. Pleaded insanity. I said, your honour, who else would park in the passing lane?' In essence, a lot of his material isn't overly funny in its own right, but his almost catatonic demeanour makes it hilarious and has earned him a cult following. Deadpan style has been used by many others, but Wright is its most prominent forerunner.

Joan Rivers became so popular she earned her own TV talk show in 1986. Rivers' stand-up style was tough-talking and often centred around satirising the lives of celebrities and public figures, as well as herself and her own Jewish background. She was often criticised for being too abrasive, but that was her style and she refused to change it. Rivers was arguably a pioneer of the modern 'roast' era. The same list from *Rolling Stone* magazine ranked her as the sixth greatest comic of all time, and her success was an inspiration for many other female comics to follow.

So many American comedians of the era made an impact that is still felt today: the fast-talking Eddie Murphy, whose videos *Raw* and *Delirious* were mandatory quoting for anyone who was cool in school, the one-liner king Rodney Dangerfield who gets 'no respect', Bill Cosby, whose sitcom was the first to portray an affluent black American family, the working class mum Roseanne Barr who became another TV star through appealing to the blue collar masses, and the observational Garry Shandling, who was a close friend and inspiration for Jerry Seinfeld. In 2016 he appeared on Jerry's TV series *Comedians in Cars Getting Coffee*, in which he explained his relationship with comedy – 'It's your spirit, your soul and your being. It's why you're on the planet.' Shandling passed away weeks later.

Meanwhile, British comedy was evolving into its own niches, just as diverse but mostly distinctive for its satirical nature and peculiarity. British humourists were first known to me through their TV roles, and as a child my earliest impression of the motherland was of three weird men riding a triseater bicycle. *The Goodies* made no sense at all, but they were amusing and an integral part of my early education on British culture. Dad also would sometimes let me stay up late to enjoy *The Two Ronnies*, but he must have grown exasperated by my frequent – and arguably hilarious – references to the *three* Ronnies, as Ron Tiffen was a Ronnie himself.

At the same time, I fell in love with *Monty Python*, particularly John Cleese and Eric Idle, who for me personified comic silliness and cynicism. I had an audio cassette of *Monty Python and the Holy Grail* and listened to it until the tape actually wore away. Listening to the audio cassette forced me to focus carefully on the delivery and nuances of the dialogue, and I found great humour in subtleties that seemed to lose their impact when viewing the movie. Soon enough, *The Young Ones* became a schoolyard phenomenon, despite the fact that none of us in early high school had any concept of its underlying political satire. We thought the hippie Neil was funny, and his filling a bag with green slime in the episode *Snot* was comedic art of the highest echelon.

But by far my greatest comedic idol, from a young age to present day, has been the incomparable Scotsman Billy Connolly. The 'Big Yin' had an outrageous potty mouth that was ahead of its time for the British stand-up and TV scene. From his early days in the 1970s he would offer a deep-thinking, constructive analysis of issues such as flatulence, defecation, urination, masturbation, sex, disease, death and the Catholic Church. He would swear a lot, but it wasn't gratuitous. Unnecessary profanity can detract from a comedy routine. Billy, however, could make your grandmother snigger.

When I discovered Billy, I loved the mirror he would hold up to society. He wouldn't often rant about politics or spend too much time on big social issues, but he could talk for five minutes about choosing a shampoo, or the grief he feels when a menu doesn't contain enough information ('You can't just say "I'll have Soup of the Day". You know, a shot in the dark. Because it might be Octopus Arsehole Soup.') A master storyteller, he would often drift into so many hilarious tangents that by the time he returned to his main anecdote we had forgotten he was even telling a story, which was part of what made it so funny. That was his definitive style – Billy admits he never did 'bits' – his entire career was based on storytelling and observation. After retiring from stand-up he said, 'I've always loved telling stories. It's the most natural thing in the world for me... I wouldn't tell jokes, as such, I told wee stories.'

He was a very physical comedian who could use every part of the stage. In one early routine he mocks a 'trendy young lad' at a nightclub wearing incontinence pants, dancing and gyrating while gradually soiling them. As he keeps dancing, his legs get heavier and the audience is roaring with laughter, which just seems to egg Billy on, in the manner of a child getting high on the attention of his mates. A kid at school would be scolded for being so silly, but when Billy does it he has thousands of dignified adults laughing until their ribs hurt, and buying his DVD.

And of course there is his wonderful, beautiful, glorious Scottish accent. I often wondered if that was what made him so funny. After all, I'm pretty sure if most Australian comics did his material word for word it would sound ridiculous. But Billy was equally adored in Scotland, where presumably he sounds just like everyone else. I think it was more his relatability that made Billy so universally loved. Sometimes you could forget he was on stage and see him as just that funny bloke at a barbecue.

One of my English teachers once asked our class to write a story about a dinner party where we could invite six famous guests. Billy Connolly was the first to get a seat at my table and was the life of the party. Batman laughed so hard Pepsi came out his nose. Elle Macpherson farted. And my teacher gave me a detention for writing 'I couldn't even remember what he was talking about, he was just really fucking funny!'

Back home in Australia, our own distinctive style of comedy was emerging. Our humourists were first known to us through radio and television, and my grandmother told the story of how she was heartbroken in November 1963 when she saw the newspaper headline 'Kennedy Assassinated', believing it to be Graham Kennedy from her beloved *In Melbourne Tonight*. 'Gra-Gra' was one of our earliest popular comedic personalities, with a classic set-up and punch style.

Two more early icons were Garry McDonald and Barry Humphries. Both were brilliant character comics, who respectively portrayed Norman Gunston – the nervous reporter with toilet paper stuck to his face to clot shaving cuts, and Dame Edna Everage – the grandiose housewife from Moonee Ponds whose 'Hellooo possums' became as Aussie as Vegemite. Australian humour from its roots emerged as a rather self-deprecating view of our character and culture, and elements of that have remained ever since. I've heard it suggested this relates to our underdog status in the world. Aussies have always been happy to take the piss out of themselves in a manner that is mocking, yet at the same time immensely proud.

It stands to reason that our most famous comedic export of the 1980s was not a comedian who toiled for years in clubs to work his way to the top, but a bloke who worked as a rigger on Sydney Harbour Bridge. Paul Hogan's mates thought he was funny and talked him into appearing on TV talent show *New Faces*. As a distant predecessor for modern talent shows, the quality of acts was not exactly high and feedback from judges would often involve comments such as, 'Mate, I'd lay off the guitar until you take some more lessons'. Inadvertently, the lampooning judges almost became the stars of the show but, unimpressed with some of their over-the-top derision towards contestants who were having a genuine crack, Hogan decided to get one back on them. The unknown rigger from working class Granville in Western Sydney appeared as a 'tap-dancing knife thrower from Lightning Ridge'. After greeting the nation with his soon to be customary 'Evening viewers', he proceeded to roast the judges in a manner unheard of on Australian TV.

'They say the camera adds ten pounds… how many cameras have you eaten?'

'Bill… I'd ask him to stand up, but he already is.'

'Rob… he's a comedian. If you say so Rob.'

Hogan then tap-danced in his work boots for a few seconds and threw his knives to the floor.

Almost overnight, this bloke in a sleeveless flannel shirt and footy shorts became our most lovable and definitive Aussie larrikin. 'Hoges' liked to laugh at authority and, as a testament to his popularity, when he once jokingly suggested to viewers they attach a ten dollar note to their tax return in order to speed up their payment, over seven thousand Australians actually did so. It's fair to observe that wasn't the last time Hoges managed to annoy the tax man – he did so in a much more publicised way a few years later after becoming the highest grossing Australian film star of his era, when *Crocodile Dundee* became an international hit – a film that led Americans to believe that all Aussies are slightly insane and live in the outback. I had a friend in high school who visited America with his family and was asked the *serious* question of whether he had wrestled a crocodile.

An integral part of any Aussie childhood was *Hey Hey It's Saturday,* which in those days was the best mainstream TV exposure local comics could get. This was where I discovered Vince Sorrenti, the son of Italian immigrants, who was loud and highly energised and allowed us to laugh at ourselves from an adopted Aussie's perspective. I once saw him in person at the St Kilda Festival, and clearly remember his 'cheese' bit, which became my favourite. As an Italian, our cheeses must have intrigued him: 'Mmm, those single slices wrapped in plastic are *sooo* nice. I'll have mine extra mild thanks, don't want to taste any of that cheese shit.'

I also loved Jimeoin, an Irishman whose first routine I remember on *Hey Hey* was all about seagulls. He pondered why they don't have eyebrows, and for the next thirty years every time I saw a seagull I wondered the same thing. And there was Shane Bourne, who lived near us in Elsternwick and always smiled and said 'G'day' when we would call out to him on the street. He did a segment called *The Great Aussie Joke* with the lovable Maurie Fields, where they would tell joke-book style anecdotes sent in by viewers. The jokes themselves wouldn't be very funny if you read them in a book, but these two could make them priceless. That's the skill of the comedian.

Maurie's son Marty Fields was to become another popular comedian who I've enjoyed watching in comedy clubs and on TV. Among many other favourites of the *Hey Hey* era were Russell Gilbert, Trevor Marmalade, Paul Calleja, Brad Oakes, Bob Franklin and a young Dave Hughes.

Another comic I cherished from early on was Elliot Goblet. I loved his deadpan style, which was possibly inspired by Steven Wright, but Elliot was more positive in his own droll manner. He had a signature goatee beard and bold-framed glasses, and I was fascinated at how he could keep such a straight face and stare down the lens of the camera, delivering each clever musing in an expressionless monotone: 'Here's an interesting fact. One in two people make up 50% of the population.' One time, I remember him being at risk of breaking character as he tried to suppress a laugh, which surely must be a regular challenge, but he recovered like a true professional. I wondered whether he would be very different in real life. Would he be much more charismatic, or was his stage persona only a mild exaggeration of a stolid demeanour?

When I was thirteen my lovely Aunty Jo took me to see *Wogs Out of Work* at the Comedy Theatre, a stage show featuring Nick Giannopoulos, Simon Palomares and Mary Coustas (aka 'Effie'). As a drama student I was in awe of experiencing sketch comedy in such a large theatre. 'Wog' humour was peaking in the 1980s, probably as a result of the children of the migration wave twenty years earlier growing up, and audiences were crying with laughter and slapping armrests. Aunty Jo and I had one of the funniest nights of our lives, and it got me wondering how racial stereotyping was normally considered unacceptable but, by contrast, can sell out theatres for weeks. On this occasion it was fine because the 'wogs' were making jokes about themselves. In the same way as Richard Pryor would make black jokes, it was a form of taking ownership of stereotypes.

For my sixteenth birthday my family took me to The Last Laugh in Collingwood, a now closed theatre restaurant that was very popular in the 1980s and '90s. There we saw one of the funniest live acts I can remember, a trio known as The Found Objects, two thirds of whom would soon be better known as one of Australia's most popular comedy duos, Lano and Woodley. Frank Woodley is perhaps Australia's best physical comedian, and his lanky goofiness at one stage had a lady at the table next to ours spitting out her soup. It's one of my favourite birthday memories with my family, and has always reinforced to me how comedy can make important nights so memorable.

As an adult, I have been inspired by the clean style of Adam Hills and the positivity he often projects. He is one of the few comedians who can joke about the Swedish Chef from *The*

Muppet Show and convey genuine warmth for the character. In fact, Adam had the thrill of interacting with the Swedish Chef live on stage at the Montreal Comedy Festival Gala in 2012, hosted by the Muppets. But it almost didn't happen. Adam has discussed his dilemma of deciding whether or not to do the gala, as they wanted him to change some of his material, but he decided that meeting the Muppets – his childhood idols – was too good an opportunity to miss. He was especially looking forward to meeting Kermit, and one of his friends made sure he didn't change his mind by eyeballing him and saying: 'Touch the fucking frog you idiot.'

As a metaphor for aspiring to reach your dreams, 'Touch the frog' became the catchphrase for Adam's popular festival show *Happyism*. A decent singer, Adam closed the show with a song imploring people to 'Touch the frog', backed by a large gospel-style group that seemed to appear from nowhere. It was an inspiring way to end a show about staying positive and happy. I love it when comedy can be a force for good, and I hope many people who saw the show went on to touch their own personal frogs.

Shortly afterwards, I was supervising my school's annual VCAL excursion to the Holocaust Museum in Elsternwick. I knew the museum to be only one street down from the ABC studios in which Adam filmed his talk show *In Gordon Street Tonight,* and as I led the students along Glenhuntly Road, I was caught off-guard as Adam walked straight past us! As he crossed the road, I halted the students and did probably the weirdest thing they have ever seen a teacher do.

'*Touch the frooog!*' I called to the man across the noisy street. Thankfully, Adam turned and gave us a smile and wave.

Carl Barron has long been one of my favourites for taking the piss. Just as early character-based comedians held up a mirror to Australian culture, Carl's stand-up is brilliant in its simplicity as he highlights our Australian quirks. In his laconic drawl he observes how 'Aussies are so understated... the bloke next to me on the plane looks at the wing on fire, looks at me, and says "That doesn't look good".'

Jim Jefferies is another great Australian I can binge-watch for hours. His style is crude and politically incorrect, but he's one of our most successful comedy exports and is particularly popular in America, where he now has his own talk show. Despite his lackadaisical persona, some of his social commentary can be quite sharp, and he holds the record for the most widely viewed routine on US gun laws, highlighting how comedy can be a powerful social influencer.

There are so many more comedians of past and present I could mention here. Much more paragraph space is deserved by the Doug Anthony Allstars, Tim Minchin, Hannah Gadsby, Tom Gleeson, Steady Eddy, Kitty Flanagan, Luke McGregor, Dave O'Neil, Anthony Morgan, Roy & HG, Matthew Hardy, Troy Kinne, Sam Simmons, Flight of the Conchords, Ross Noble, Dylan Moran, Jimmy Carr, Kevin Bridges, Sean Lock, Arj Barker, Russell Peters, Louis C.K, Bill Burr and Mitch Hedberg – to name but a *few*. When I truly look back upon all of the funny people who have in equal parts entertained and inspired me over my life, the list is much longer than I ever would have guessed. But that's a wonderful testament to the depth and breadth of comedic talent that touches our lives.

I can't help but wonder how less interesting life might have been without these people. And I'm sure there are still plenty of amazingly good comedians, famous or not, that I haven't discovered yet. So when people ask me who my favourites are (a common question lately), I like to answer briefly and flip it back on the person who asked, because any comedians that have inspired others enough to be brought into such a conversation are surely worth knowing about.

And as for my very earliest comedic influence as a child? Well, I shared Adam Hills' passion for *The Muppet Show*, so I must admit I deeply adored and drew inspiration from the incomparable Fozzie Bear. He had a residency on the show despite rarely getting laughs. Fozzie's material was actually woeful, but he kept trying, bringing a different set every night. That's what I admired about him, he *persevered*. With regularity he'd be heckled, normally by Statler and Waldorf, the two grumpy old men in the balcony, but he held his head high and kept faith in himself despite those who were intent on bringing him down.

Fozzie himself drew inspiration from the unsighted Gags Beasley, writer of the infamous 'banana sketch' that Fozzie and other members of the cast could never repeat because they would be laughing too much to ever get it out. I liked this element of character depth, that even a Muppet comedian had others who inspired him.

Of all the comics who have achieved fame, from the vaudeville era to Netflix, there wouldn't be a single one who hasn't done the Fozzie Bear apprenticeship. Like any craft, it takes years of gruelling hard yards to truly succeed. And as comedy has evolved around the world, and continues to evolve in so many wonderful and diverse directions, the one element shared by so many of its famous practitioners has been the extraordinary toil that has gone into their craft.

Only upon reflection has it really hit me how much of a role comedy has played in my life. My journey into it so far had barely started, but like most things that are worth achieving, I was feeling motivated to put in the work. There was undoubtedly some intense work to come, but when I looked back at the value that comedy had already added to my life – and the world – I figured it's not a bad thing to be involved in.

I booked a third gig at Station 59 for the earliest possible date.

5

FIFTEEN SECONDS

For my third attempt at stand-up I did something a bit sneaky – I didn't tell anyone about it. I disliked being secretive, but I felt this would take the pressure off and allow me to relax a bit more on stage. As much as I valued support from family and friends, for now I definitely needed some 'me' time.

What I wasn't expecting as I turned up alone to Station 59 was how incredibly crowded it was going to be. As I swung open the door, my heart skipped a beat. It was definitely standing room only, and the sheer volume of conversation created a wall of noise that immediately sickened me to the gut. Who were all these people and why were they at my gig? As it turned out, I'd booked myself a spot for the last show of the year before the Christmas break, which was popular for many comics and fans of the venue. It was going to be an absolute hoot. But I didn't *want* a hoot! I desperately wanted an easy night. I'd been feeling more confident since getting laughs at my second performance, and I was optimistic about some new material I'd been working on, but how could I possibly relax in front of a full house? Again, my mind chose to ignore the positives. For example, tonight's audience was mostly punters (a common term for those who turn up simply to watch the show, as opposed to other performers – the more punters in a crowd the better) and the fact that larger crowds can naturally lead to bigger laughs. Instead, all I could focus on was that a silence from sixty or more people would be more embarrassing than a silence from ten.

Before jostling my way to the bar to place a tick beside my name on the set list, my mind flashed back to my first gig. The same butterflies pounded my stomach and I seriously considered just bailing. Nobody had come to see me, and there were so many comedians on the list tonight that my absence would barely be noticed. It would be so easy to just slip out and go home, feet up in front of the TV within an hour, relaxing and letting my mind go numb. For a moment I gave this serious consideration, but eventually decided *no*, that would go against everything I had told myself lately. Staying off the couch and out of my comfort zone was the key to this journey. Plus, Kieran was now back from Edinburgh so tonight would be his first observation of me and I felt a strong urge to impress him. He was a true advocate for comedy. He didn't run a room to give himself stage time, he ran it to support the artform and give comedic artists a voice. Station 59 was a comedy community, the first I had become a marginal part of, and I really wanted to thank Kieran by contributing well to what was now seeming like a big event.

After saying hello to some regulars, for the third time in a row I felt the need to go for a walk outside in order to mentally run through my routine. At this early stage I very much wanted to remember every word. Some comics seemed to be able to interact with the crowd from the outset, but I was nowhere near that yet and my greatest fear was not so much silence after a punchline, but forgetting material altogether. I'd been proud and mildly surprised so far to get through my first two gigs without forgetting anything. It was interesting how all of my words had naturally come to mind while standing under the spotlights. Still, I did not yet consider that to be anything but a fluke, and my pre-show ritual was becoming important.

With ten minutes or so before the show, I stepped outside and slowly ambled down Church Street, uttering every word of my routine beneath my breath, hitting key syllables in the right places. I didn't want my routine to be a memory test, but in order for it to work I had to pretty much get every word, every inflection, just right. While concentrating, I wasn't paying much attention to the street and at one stage a young man with a glazed look walked past me. He appeared quite detached from his surroundings and seemed to be murmuring to himself. At first I thought nothing of it, as the drug users of this part of Richmond were a constant source of material for local comics. Near the end of Church Street, I turned and walked back towards the pub. The spaced-out man had turned as well and was now walking towards me again. I took my hands out of my pockets as an instinct. We crossed paths once more and this time made brief eye contact, and I saw a look that I wasn't expecting. He didn't look stoned or aggravated: his brow was furrowed in concentration. In fact, he looked slightly familiar. Hang on, was this guy one of my own? And is that what I looked like to others? As I returned to the pub there was another guy, taller with long hair, sucking the life out of a cigarette and pacing the footpath. He too seemed to be having a conversation within his mind and I recognised him as another new comic who had debuted last week. Perhaps Richmond didn't have a drug problem after all. Perhaps its main problem was amateur comedians!

Back inside I grabbed a beer and was soon greeted by the guy who minutes earlier I'd thought might have mugged me. We shook hands and both laughed at our common predicament. It was comforting to know I wasn't the only nervous person in the room. He was a top bloke and I now feel awful that I don't remember his name (why is it I can remember the names of a hundred students, but introduce yourself to me while I'm preparing for a comedy gig and it will just bounce off my ears?) We had a good chat and it was great to relieve the nerves a little.

'I had a feeling you were another comedian,' he said. 'You do the same walk as me before a gig.'

'Good to know,' I laughed. 'Then there was the guy on the corner as well.'

'We must look like zombies!'

'Have you done many gigs?' I asked.

'This is my second. First one was here as well. You?'

'Third, all here.'

We chatted for a bit and he introduced me to another guy, about ten years younger than me with the lean physique of a footballer. He had reddish hair and wore a tight grey T-shirt, one that I couldn't wear as my abs had disappeared years ago. He was immediately likeable. Now the three of us were in this together.

The show started punctually and with so many comics on the bill it was likely to plough right through with no interval. (Whether or not open mic shows take a 'ten-minute' break normally depends on how many comics there are or, more to the point, whether or not the MC is a smoker. If so, a lengthy break is assured, which often results in a smaller audience for the second half. But tonight Station 59 was sure to be full steam ahead with no break and the seven-minute limit strictly enforced.)

Kieran got the room laughing straight away with some solid warm up material, and then his standard opening before the first act:

> Kieran: 'How much are the comedians getting paid tonight?'
>
> Crowd: 'Fuck all!'
>
> Kieran: 'And how much did you pay to get in here tonight?'
>
> Crowd: 'Fuck all!'
>
> Kieran: 'That's right… so ladies and gentlemen, please make sure you pay all of our comedians tonight with your love, your attention and, most of all, your laughter.'

The first few acts were great and the room was well-charged. The night began as a rollicking show like I hadn't experienced here before, with people clearly unwinding leading into their holiday breaks. I should have been pleased about this, as the best rooms in which to perform are clearly ones full of laughing people, however for some reason it was only making me more nervous. Perhaps I was terrified of being the only one to bomb. (Public speaking, remember, is a greater fear than death.) Despite this, I was happy to see the night going so well, as Kieran and Station 59 had been a big part of my life in 2013 and they deserved a big finish to the year.

Unlike most comedy room runners, Kieran doesn't use a fixed set list. Comedians would only know their set was coming up when he tapped them on the shoulder two acts in advance. This had the benefit of keeping comics in the room and attentive. Plus, Kieran was a great reader of audiences. He could read the peaks and troughs of a comedy crowd like a surfer could read waves. When the room needed someone high on energy to pick it up, he would find the right act. When the time was right for a more relaxed, storytelling-type comedian, again he would find the right act. And he would spread out his rookies. He would normally allow a newbie like me to get up after somebody solid in order to piggyback a bit off their laughs. This was a great method, but the downside for me was that it kept my routine on a loop in my mind. If I knew how long I had to wait, I could relax and enjoy some of the other acts for a while. Instead I was always mentally ten minutes from getting up. At about the one hour mark I got the tap. This was relatively early and the room was just as full as it had been at the start. People were still laughing, nobody had really bombed, and in a familiar way my heartbeat accelerated rapidly.

I was beginning to believe that waiting to get called up onto a comedy stage was the most excruciating wait imaginable. Sure, if you're pulled aside at an Indonesian airport strapped with nine kilograms of cocaine the wait could be worse, but only a little. Here there could be somebody speaking on stage directly in front of you, yet you will have no comprehension of what they are saying. A 40cm raised platform in the corner of a Richmond pub will suddenly feel like the concert stage at Rod Laver Arena just down the road. As I experienced this sickening feeling once more, I had a dire moment in which I questioned how I'd even found myself here in the first place. The Ben Tiffen I knew was not a stand-up comedian. The guy I had always known, at least the adult version of him, was shy and self-conscious around new people and absolutely did not belong on stage in a noisy, crowded pub. At this moment, I felt the biggest stab of self-doubt of my life. As I manoeuvred my way towards the front of the room to find a clear pathway to the stage, I began to question why I was putting myself through this. Surely there were easier hobbies, like cliff diving or swimming with sharks.

'Yadda yadda yadda,' is roughly what I remember of Kieran's introduction, 'Yadda yadda… Ben Tiffen!'

I stepped up to much louder and more enthusiastic applause than I'd expected, obviously just the momentum of the night, and launched passionately into the same opening I'd used last time by proclaiming that I was 'in love'. Even though I'd only heard one person laugh the first time, I figured it had been a big laugh in a small crowd and if I delivered it with more passion and confidence, a larger crowd would hopefully react well. At first, a good section of the audience responded, which was encouraging, and I proceeded to the punchline: 'However, I know there are fourteen steps to her bedroom window.' There were some minor laughs from different parts of the pub, but certainly not what I'd been hoping for from such a lively crowd.

'Ha!' said one person towards the front before stopping abruptly, as though embarrassed to be the only one laughing at his table.

I couldn't go immediately into my next bit as it wouldn't have flowed well enough, so I had to tolerate a few seconds of painful silence. Most comics usually have a line prepared for moments when a punchline doesn't hit – a 'save' that can at least score a laugh by making fun of the joke itself – but I didn't even have that yet. And to make it worse, I had even less confidence in my next punchline.

'Oh no, not again!' said my brain.

Perhaps I'd been deluding myself all along. Perhaps I'd been over-confident and I was never destined to be funny on stage. As the entire room looked at me expectantly, I lost whatever confidence I'd managed to muster.

'You're out of your depth,' said the little voice in my mind, and I genuinely considered walking off. I'd seen a few rookie comics do so on this very stage. To quit is no big deal, really. Comedy is such a tough gig, sometimes just standing up and having a go can be reward enough and nobody ever begrudges a walk off. In fact, I've seen some walk offs get more encouraging applause than bad gigs. There would be no shame right now in just thanking the crowd and leaving to find a less humiliating hobby. I surely couldn't endure another six and a half minutes of failed punchlines.

But something compelled me to keep going, at least for one more joke. I'd made it this far, I might as well give it everything. So I held my nerve and continued undaunted, which, I was to find out later, is exactly the advice true professionals follow. Never dwell on bits that miss, just move the show forward and they can be quickly forgotten.

'Got myself this cool new iPhone,' I announced proudly. 'Just by a show of hands, how many people here tonight have ever camped out for a new phone?' No takers, which suited my set-up. 'None of you? Good response. Who are these losers camping overnight in shopping centres just for a phone?' This actually got a bigger laugh than I'd thought, and some cheers of agreement. 'I mean, you see them on the news [act out] "Ohh it's got a brighter screen"... Yeah – brighter than your future, dickhead!'

Bang! Big laugh.

In fact, a surprisingly big laugh. It almost felt like the whole room laughing as one, the way I'd always imagined it. Finally, I heard what I'd been aspiring to all this time. I was immediately reinvigorated! And weirdly this wasn't even a punchline I'd rated highly. I'd spent much more time writing other material that had flopped. But to my eternal relief this simple line worked well. Reading it on paper it didn't look that funny, but most jokes don't. In performance, however, I'd delivered it with angst. Eventually this gig was to set two patterns in my comedy journey – the first being that some of my best material would be bits I didn't rate well when I first wrote them. It took me a while to figure out what audiences would best react to.

I steered into a discussion on how modern smart devices had provided such wondrous advancements for humankind, yet of all their amazing applications, perhaps the most predictable had been freer access to porn. I highlighted the irony that every time the human race advances we find ways to act like cavemen again. This got some initial laughs, but then I put a twist on my concerns by bemoaning that such easy access to soft porn wasn't around when I was a teenager and kids today don't know how easy they've got it.

'My generation had to work for these things!' I rued, explaining that just as each generation before us would complain about how much harder life was for them, this was our adversity. The crowd came with me on this and for the first time I could palpably feel the trust building. I lamented the amount of work my mates and I would go to at the newsagent after school 'just to sneak a peek at a black-and-white topless picture on page three of *The Truth*'. More big laughs, which continued as I related my first experience of seeing nudity on TV when a streaker made a surprise appearance in the 1982

VFL Grand Final (and to this day, I maintain she cost my team Richmond a premiership). Seeing football and a naked woman together had been way too much for my nine year-old brain to process at the time, I explained, however a few years later it was odd that the tracking on our old VHS recording of the game went suspiciously distorted around the eleven-minute mark of the third quarter. I caught a glimpse of Kieran at this stage, and he was genuinely laughing with the rest of the crowd. It can be hard to make comedy experts laugh but, as a footy fanatic of my era, he related to this material. I was thrilled to make Kieran laugh among all others on this big night. With the crowd behind me, some other new bits I'd written continued to hit just as well.

I stepped off stage to a full round of applause which this time seeped into my bones. Weeks of trial and error had gone into those last seven minutes and, despite an awkward opening, I had made a room full of people laugh for a few minutes of their lives. Nobody had any inkling of the mental gymnastics I'd just been through to turn an almost terminal moment into one of my proudest. Maybe I had potential in this caper after all. When Kieran took back the mic, he followed up with some further views and gags on the 1982 VFL Grand Final, which felt like a wonderful endorsement.

I also discovered that the walk through the crowd after a successful gig is an amateur comedian's fifteen seconds of fame. In fact, to make the most self-indulgent statement of my life, as I strode up to the bar I almost felt like a celebrity. *Yes, I know how ridiculous that sounds!* However, I couldn't help but enjoy the fantasy. The moments after a successful gig, where relief flushes through you and you receive the plaudits of other comics and punters alike, is one of the pay-offs for amateur comedians. I guessed this was part of the buzz that keeps comedians hooked. I'd heard some describe comedy as addictive and I was beginning to understand why.

'Great set, man,' said a voice behind me at the bar. I turned to find Tony Magnuson, the *Ghost* guy.

'Oh, thanks mate!'

'I've added you on Facebook,' he noted, pocketing his phone. Of all things that can make you feel loved these days! This felt like my first true moment of acceptance into the community, and Tony was to become one of my first real comedian friends. We chatted for a while and a nicer bloke you will truly never meet.

'So I was shitting myself after my first bit bombed,' I admitted, 'but luckily I pulled it back.'

'Yeah, you did well man. The stalker bit was a bit predictable.'

'Oh, really?'

He explained that the premise and twist was a bit old. And he recommended that I shouldn't position myself to be a creep. The humour in a joke like that would best come from highlighting how I didn't *understand* how my behaviour was wrong (this was the technique of the comic flaw). I could develop this routine further if I wanted to, but for now I decided to put it aside and keep focusing on what had just worked well.

Following me was the sporty guy in the grey T-shirt. I was amazed at how comfortable he looked and how engaging he was from the beginning. In fact, his natural ease and energy almost knocked my newly found confidence down a notch. He was getting laugh after laugh and I immediately aspired to be more like him. But still, I'd taken another big step, which again was due to pushing myself at times when I felt like giving up. In a sense I felt as though I'd arrived tonight, and I wanted to feel that buzz again and again.

The only downside was that no family or friends were there to see it. This would become the second frustrating pattern of my comedy journey — for a long time my best gigs were habitually missed by them. But perhaps leaving them at home had been the key to loosening up a bit on stage. Either way, it didn't worry me too much at present, because if I was going anywhere with this comedy thing, they would have plenty more opportunities to see me. (However, it would have been heartening to hear Matthew's post-gig analysis on the drive home.)

I definitely wanted more stage time, and as Station 59 was taking a Christmas break it was time to venture beyond the familiarity of my new favourite pub and boldly explore the diversity of Melbourne's huge amateur comedy scene. So much more opportunity awaited, and I wanted a new challenge sooner rather than later.

6
THE NEXT STEPS

It's surprising to discover how many amateur comedy events exist in Melbourne when you take the time to research and ask around. It's a wonderful thriving scene that sneaks under the radar a bit, but now that I was making friends and becoming more of an insider, there seemed to be a number of choices pretty much every night of the week. Some were better than others, of course, but all seemed to be run by devotees of comedy motivated by passion. Melbourne has had a few professional comedy clubs come and go – the biggest and most popular at present being The Comic's Lounge – but the hardcore comedy culture of America has never quite taken off here, so in true Aussie style it's normally in the corner of good pubs all over town that you'll find some of Melbourne's funniest people and those trying to join their ranks.

Mad Dog Comedy was an open mic night at a pub called Dancing Dog Cafe in the western suburb of Footscray. Unlike Station 59 it was not necessary to book in advance, so I turned up the following Tuesday and signed up for an instant spot. There were normally many acts to get through so there was a five-minute limit and performers would get 'the light' when their time was up. The light, normally from a phone or small torch, was common to many venues, and a growing pet peeve of mine was when comics blatantly disregarded it. If they were funny it wasn't too bad, but those who pushed well beyond the flashing light with long-winded monologues that were not getting laughs could make some open mic nights arduous. *Mad Dog* was a great venue, but with a long set list it often suffered from too many comics with 'sticky feet', as it was known. For some it felt as though it almost became a game, to see how long they could sustain audience boredom with little attempt to be funny. From adversity, however, comes strength, and one of the first bits of advice I gave myself was to never treat stage time as though it's *yours*. I decided from early on that stage time does not belong to the comedian – it is the audience's time you are occupying, so you need to respect it. I've always liked to practise my sets with a stopwatch, as I consider timing to be an important comedic skill in its own right. I think this mindset helped me greatly from the beginning.

For my first gig at *Mad Dog* I basically repeated my successful set from the previous week at Station 59, minus the awkward opening. I was looking forward to getting big laughs again, but was surprised, in fact pretty shattered, when I didn't. I got a few decent chuckles in the right places, but certainly not to the point where the whole room was laughing as one. 'Damn it!' I thought, as my ego took another plunge. And in that instant I learned one of the truest lessons in comedy – just because a set works well once, doesn't mean it always will. There are many factors that go into making a comedy set work, and I was only beginning my journey towards figuring that out. For starters, this seemed to be a mostly younger crowd of twenty-somethings, as opposed to Station 59 which had a broader mix. I had to remind myself I was twice the age of some of these people and anecdotes about the 1982 VFL Grand Final probably reached their ears in the same way anecdotes about Woodstock would reach mine. I immediately became conscious of writing material that appeals to as wide an audience as possible. I've heard many open mic comics blame a poor set on the audience being 'too young' or 'too blokey', yet I've never heard those excuses from a professional. Good comedians know how to write material with fairly universal appeal.

So did that mean I should drop this material and focus on more contemporary topics? That would be a safe approach. But when I thought about it, the subject of my material that had worked so well last time was not specifically the 1982 Grand Final, it was the changing face of technology, which is always a contemporary topic. Perhaps all it needed was some tinkering. For starters, I had to ensure I was using inclusive language. Expressions such as 'Does anyone remember...?' excluded too many people. I had to tell this story of my childhood through the lens of the modern day. I rewrote it, and the next time I used it in front of a younger audience it worked well. I was finding that sometimes a bit of subtle rewriting could make a major difference. And I was particularly glad to save this bit as it was my first authentically personal story. After many, many hours of sitting through comedy, I observed that by far the most engaging material was anecdotal and personal. Vince Sorrenti doing jokes about growing up Italian in Australia is genuinely personal. Hannah Gadsby doing jokes about coming out as a lesbian is genuinely personal. A forty year old bloke doing jokes about bird shit is not. But perhaps that same bloke telling jokes about his growing pains as a teenager in the 1980s was genuinely personal, even if his biggest ordeal was the difficulty of sneaking a peek at a black and white photo in *The Truth*, and the audience was better positioned to empathise knowing that it at least appeared to be true. With this in mind, this material and other anecdotes began to work much more reliably, and showing a bit more of myself was what helped a lot of it to finally click.

Apart from *Mad Dog* there were plenty of other good venues, including *Guerrilla Comedy* at the Resistance Bar & Cafe in Hawthorn. Set in a small basement, the audience would lounge on bean bags or sit on milk crates, and if you missed out on a cushion you'd end up with a painful condition known as waffle-arse. *Guerrilla* is like performing in a teenager's bedroom, but it became one of my favourites.

Once I got to know people I was finding it pretty easy to get stage time, either by signing up on the night or booking spots in advance. Over this time, through getting up again and again, I could feel my confidence rising and I continued to expand my anecdotal material (one popular routine regarded revising your dreams as you turn forty – I used to dream about wearing the baggy green for my country, but now my only dream left was to take a catch at the cricket wearing a KFC bucket on my head). I would still get nervous before spots, but it was more out of desire to do a good job than a fear of making a complete goose of myself. And I could perceive myself slowly getting better, relatively speaking, every time I stepped up.

By the time I'd done about thirty open mic spots, friends and family began to refer to me as a comedian, which didn't sit well with me at all. It implies one is accomplished, and I'm not sure at what point that happens. While I was progressing well and finally hearing good, regular laughter with much fewer bombs, my material and stagecraft were still nowhere near the standard of others who had done hundreds of gigs, so I felt the term didn't apply to me yet and I asked people not to use it too liberally.

'But you get up on a stage and tell jokes,' a friend explained, 'that makes you a comedian.'

Fair point, I suppose. If a comedian is someone who is willing to occasionally get up on a small stage and say stuff that hopefully makes a small number of people laugh, then I guess that was me. But the word did not yet seem to allow for degrees of *comedianship*. Other words such as 'musician' can be used much more freely – it is possible for a recreational guitarist to be identified as a musician without instant comparisons to Jimi Hendrix and questions about whether you're on the telly. 'Comedian' is not quite there yet. It suggests professionalism, which is odd because most comedians do it only as a hobby.

Once I was a comedian on TV. In 2014 I appeared on a Channel Seven quiz show, *Million Dollar Minute*. I've always been a secret fanatic of quiz shows; to date I've appeared on four, and I'm sure it's because my head is incredibly full of useless facts. I don't consider myself overly intelligent, just retentive of baubles of knowledge that have no other outlet than quiz shows or trivia nights. I remember practically nothing from several years of studying French and Geography in school, yet I can recite every word from dozens of TV theme songs of the same era, and could name every Norm Smith medallist in history. I could have correctly answered the first million dollar question on the American version of *Who Wants to be a Millionaire*, because I remembered that Jethro Tull controversially beat Metallica to win the 1989 Grammy for best new hard rock or heavy metal album. I would by now struggle to do long division without a calculator, and I have no idea how anything with more than about five moving parts works, but I can tell you that Richard Nixon's middle name was Milhous, the hashtag symbol (#) is called an octothorpe, and wombats are the only animal to produce cubed poo. That's why quiz shows hold no fear for me. I wouldn't be perturbed to challenge a Mensa genius on commercial TV, for what does IQ matter when facing a question about wombat shit?

There was no studio audience at this taping (the applause is all 'canned'), so I was feeling surprisingly calm when the cameras started rolling. To begin the show, host Simon Reeve chatted to me and the other two contestants for the getting-to-know-you bit, which is important for quiz shows because viewers like to connect with the contestants. Simon looked at me with an excited arch of eyebrows.

'So Ben, I see you're a comedian?'

Arghh! I must have put something about it on the form I filled in three months ago.

'Ah, yes, Simon, yes I am.'

'Do you have your own show? Where can we see you perform?'

'Oh no, I do open mic spots around Melbourne, it's just a bit of fun really, I wouldn't call myself an actual comedian…'

'That's fantastic. Are you hoping to turn professional soon?'

'No, I just do it for fun, Simon, I'm not really a…'

'Well, good luck with your comedy career, and good luck today. Hopefully you'll be *laughing* all the way to the bank.'

HAHAHA! What witty banter. At least none of that riveting conversation made it to air. Turns out I wasn't interesting enough for viewers to get to know. I came second to the fast finishing carry-over champ and won nothing, not even a board game.

That show was soon axed and replaced by *The Chase,* hosted by Andrew O'Keefe, which I appeared on as well. On this show there is more opportunity for casual chat, and at one point I made a friendly joke directed at our opponent nicknamed 'The Beast'. Filmed in the same studio, again there was no audience, so watching my episode I was pleasantly surprised to hear a laughter sound effect following my joke. While I've always derided canned laughter, I must admit I was mildly thrilled because it meant someone, somewhere, in a position of authority, had decided that the air after my joke could not possibly be silent. The words coming from my mouth on national television had been judged worthy of at least second-hand laughter. Again, I won nothing. But it was worth it.

Annoyingly, some friends began to take great pride in introducing me to new people as a comedian, and the reaction upon meeting me in this manner was always the same – an excited surprise, followed by a scrutinising of my face and a look of disappointment upon realising I'm nobody famous. Of course, within minutes someone would ask me to tell a joke, leaving me to look extraordinarily unfunny as I explain, 'It doesn't work like that'. Likewise, on occasions when I was socially funny, inevitably the call would come: 'Oh, the comedian! Here we go, he's doing a routine!'

At the same time, odd behaviour began to ensue from work colleagues. For some reason, many seemed to think I was sourcing material directly from them, as though comedians simply get up on stage to make fun of those they interact with during any given day. One lady, a lovely educational support worker, once bumped into another staff member in the tea room and spilled her drink. Not the worst thing to happen, but she was embarrassed and as she cleaned the mess there was the inevitable cajoling to 'Use that in one of your routines!' As usual, I smiled politely and laughed along with the joke, maybe even sarcastically suggesting that I would. Later that day, I'd well and truly forgotten the moment when the dear lady approached me and whispered 'Please don't use that in your routine'. My heart broke at the thought she had spent the whole day worrying that I would!

As anyone in comedy can relate to, 'You should use that in a routine' is one of the most tiresome comments you will hear. In a similar way, in an early *Seinfeld* episode, a man at a party grabs Jerry's arm and says, 'Watch what you say to this guy – he'll put it in his next act!' Jerry smiles and nods with false politeness, and I'm certain this is an in-joke for fellow comics.

I can understand how it would be a natural thing to say to somebody whose hobby is to get on stage and often make fun of others – it just gets a tad repetitive. And the next most repetitive line is, 'How do you deal with hecklers?'

While there seems to be a belief that stand-up comedy is all about swatting away hecklers, as I progressed on the open mic scene I was finding heckling to be relatively rare. I'm sure that's because most open mic venues are reasonably supportive and heckling is discouraged. Of course, there is often banter between audience and comic, which can keep one on their toes, but genuine heckling of the hostile kind was not common. I've heard horror stories about bigger, more professional venues around Melbourne and Sydney in the 1980s and '90s where preparing for a gig was like preparing for combat. To be abused on stage was considered a rite of passage. Thankfully, I had not needed to deal with anything like that yet.

Only a few times early on did I witness heckling. The first was, ironically, of perhaps the physically largest comic I've ever seen. I can't remember his name but he clearly lifted weights twice daily and looked like Ivan Drago from *Rocky IV*. I would have been too scared to text during his set, let alone heckle. He was at Station 59 indulging in what was continuing to be my most dreaded form of amateur comedy, the political rant. I don't mind ranting if it's funny, but some use their stage time to simply vent, and this was a classic example of a performer who considered humour to be just an optional extra for a comedy set. This guy was ranting passionately about then-Prime Minister Tony Abbott and I'm sure the only thing keeping the audience from getting up was fear. At eight minutes he'd already exceeded his allotted time, with no hint of slowing down, when a small Irishman who was slumped over a table like a bored schoolboy sprang to life and cried 'This isn't a fucking Michael Moore documentary! Try some comedy!' A stunned silence filled the room. For a second, Drago looked dazed. Then he glared down at his verbal assailant as though he was about to eat him. Undeterred, the young bloke added, 'People come here to laugh, brother!' It's no wonder, I thought, that jokes about Irishmen are a genre of their own.

After a tense moment the strangest thing happened. Drago simply mumbled a thank you, cradled the microphone back into its stand and skulked off stage looking decidedly hurt. The luck of the Irish was with the young lad this night. But what struck me was that Drago seemed offended by the criticism of his *material*. What had seemed like a meaningless rant had actually meant a lot to him. He'd put work into it. And it highlighted to me that no matter how off the mark some comics may seem, there can still be a lot of passion and personal investment that goes into so much of what is performed on the small stage. The MC of the evening spoke to Drago supportively, and to the Irishman about comedy etiquette and how heckling was discouraged. I think they eventually shook hands, and the Irishman was challenged to come back the next week to perform his own act for the first time. I returned the following week and he was actually quite good.

Another time at Station 59, I was enjoying watching a very impressive young comic named Luka Muller. His set was going well until an aggressive drunken slur was hurled at him from the back of the room. It was hard to decipher any words except for *'fuckin''* a couple of times, but still it stopped the show. Luka peered through the lights to identify the aggressor, welcoming the challenge, until he realised it was an old man on a mobility scooter. As the crowd turned, the man lurched forward like a learner driver bunny-hopping his father's car and threw another drunken barb at the young comic. Luka seemed lost for words. Perhaps Jim Jefferies might get away with taking down a disabled heckler, but Luka was at least nice enough to hesitate. Before anyone could think of something to say the old bloke spun around, ranting loudly, and performed somewhat of a burnout. He throttled towards the exit and crashed through the swinging doors like the Ghost Train at Luna Park. The room watched in stunned silence for a moment and then with barely a further word returned to the performance. The old bloke was picked up later that night for starting a fight at the Vine Hotel down the road. Michael, as I learned his name to be, was 'known to police'.

Through some other observations, I was beginning to believe the first important rule when dealing with hecklers was to identify a heckle in the first place. I witnessed some comedians fire up at audience members who were simply interacting. Perhaps they were overzealous and too ready for a battle, but it became clear that an easy way to lose an audience was to be overly aggressive towards a perceived heckler who was just taking part in the show. People who come to comedy shows generally understand they are allowed to be a part of it. In fact, these are the type of people you want in your audience. To cut them down unnecessarily means they may quickly dislike you. However, when the heckle thrown at the comic is genuinely aggressive or nasty, the game can be on. To begin with, to even dignify the assailant as a heckler requires some discernment. To paraphrase world-famous Aussie comic Steve Hughes, the badge of 'heckler' should be reserved only for those who are funny and witty. He observes that most audience members shouting out should be considered nothing more than drunken bozos who are easy to take down, however an interaction with a genuine heckler – a funny battle of wits – can be much more interesting. And while a lot of what may transpire is spontaneous and relies upon the skill of the comedian, many will still have an arsenal of lines prepared for the occasion. I was already considering carrying one in my back pocket and committing it to memory. Sometimes, believe it or not, comedians actually *welcome* hecklers, as it opens a whole new avenue for laughter. At times it can help the performer achieve some big laughs after a bit that might have fallen flat, the perfect spot for a heckler to impose themselves. Some of the funniest moments I've witnessed of professional comedians are their put downs of hecklers, and for the audience it adds an element of spontaneity and uniqueness to their show. Like so many other challenges in comedy, I knew that dealing with hecklers would be one I would eventually need to embrace rather than shy away from, even if it was so far out of my comfort zone it couldn't be sighted without a powerful telescope.

I guess my greatest fear in being heckled would be the ultimate indignity of the heckler being funnier than me. The more I thought about it, the more I began to collect heckler comebacks and put downs as they came to me, taking pride in them but at the same time hoping they would never be needed.

By Easter time, as the Melbourne International Comedy Festival (MICF) rolled around, I would have been extremely keen to see a wide variety of acts – several of which, by now, were performed by people I knew personally. But first I had another destination in mind. As a late fortieth birthday present to myself, I was about to address another bucket list item. I was flying to America for the school holidays. I'd never been to the USA and I couldn't wait to finally check it out. My itinerary was Los Angeles, San Francisco and Las Vegas. I would have dearly loved to see more, including New York, but was content to save that for a future trip in order to relax and take my time enjoying the west coast first.

And of course, the first thing I Googled in LA was open mic comedy venues.

7

THE GOLDEN STATE

California. Has there ever been a place with more songs written about it? A quick search reveals hundreds of common songs about America's most populous state, inspiring images of driving down the 101, flying away to Malibu, Santa Monica dreaming, dark desert highways, Sunset Boulevard, a city of angels and – at least according to the Beach Boys – the cutest girls in the world. Even to those like myself who had never been there, Cali seemed to have its own soul. An ideology of freedom. It seemed a decent way to spend the school holidays.

A mind-blowing statistic is that if the state of California was its own country, it would be the fifth largest economy in the world. The *fifth*. And nothing says more about this wonderfully diverse state with a booming economy than the fact that for several years its governor was Arnold Schwarzenegger.

To be clear, I'm a massive Arnie fan. I always admire someone who can rise to the top of their field through many years of hard work and determination. As a teenager I bought his book *Arnold's Bodybuilding for Men* with dreams of sculpting my adolescent frame into something more awe-inspiring. But like so many other copies of this book, I'm sure, it turned out to be nothing more than just an interesting read. I'm a big fan of his action films, such as the *Terminator* series, *Predator* and *True Lies*, but my real love of Arnie came from his almost seamless transition into comedy. While it was obvious that the commercial Hollywood machine was manufacturing easy hilarity by placing the world's most formidable action hero into fish-out-of-water roles such as kindergarten teacher or the world's first pregnant man, I thought Arnold nailed these roles well, with a degree of subtlety to his humour that defied expectations. Some fellow actors lambasted Arnold's acting ability, however I would challenge any of them to suddenly change careers and become Mr Universe.

The irony of the world's most famous bodybuilder evolving into the 'Governator' was best surmised by Irish comedian Dylan Moran:

> 'Do you know how he got into that position? He got there by lifting things... He went right over to the heavy thing and lifted it, and put it down again. He didn't move it anywhere. And then he lifted it again, hundreds of times... Now that sounds a little dim. But it was they who said "You're the man. You're the one we want to deal with immigration, and water rates, and taxes and all that kind of shit".'

That, to me, typifies California. Before even setting foot there, I could tell it was a place I needed to see.

I can never sleep on airplanes, even long hauls across the Pacific. I get quite resentful of those who can snuggle comfortably into a pillow and wake peacefully in a new continent; my first view of any new country is normally through a very dense brain fog.

This time, however, I didn't go straight to bed, as the excitement of exploring a new place as vibrant as Los Angeles was too much to resist, so I headed immediately to Hollywood Boulevard, near my hotel, to check out the famous Star Walk.

This street has the problem of many tourists walking around with their heads down looking for the star of their favourite actors on the pavement. I did exactly the same thing and found one of mine, Harrison Ford, outside Foot Locker, and promptly cleaned the pigeon poo off him before getting one of the oddest selfies I've ever taken, with a piece of footpath. Then I checked out the celebrity footprints and signatures in the cement outside the Chinese Theatre, the venue in which many blockbuster movies have premiered. While doing so I was approached by a young man in bright clothing, a big set of headphones and plenty of bling. He greeted me warmly and asked where I was from. When I told him 'Melbourne, Australia', he beamed and offered his hand in that way that's halfway between a handshake and a high-five that made me feel very cool. Gee, Americans can be quite friendly, I thought, to greet someone so nicely when they look like they are alone and from out of town. I was very impressed!

'I've performed at the Big Day Out in Melbourne,' he explained.

'Oh wow, I've been to a few of those,' I replied truthfully. 'What do you do?'

'Here, check it out.' He placed his headphones on me and dropped a beat. It sounded good, but to my ears it sounded like any other electronic dance music, and I had no idea how to comment on it.

'It's not really my type of music, mate,' I explained, 'but it sounds great – well done.'

'Here man, take one of my CDs as a souvenir,' he said, removing the headphones and placing an unlabelled disc in my hands.

'No worries… thanks,' I said, taking the CD to be polite. I made to leave, saying, 'Nice to meet you, have a great day now.' But he wasn't ready to end the conversation.

'You see, I'm a recording artist. Most people make a donation for the CD of, like, five dollars.'

Now I saw where this was going. I didn't really want to give him a 'donation', but I was growing increasingly tired and keen to head back to my hotel. And, to be honest, there was part of me that was just pleased to have talked to somebody, so I gave him a fiver and we parted with another cool handshake of sorts.

As I walked away, I considered that I'd just paid five American dollars for a burnt CD of music that I didn't like from a guy who probably was not a recording artist and had simply researched music festivals from popular tourist countries. But still, I'd made a new friend and acquired, at the very least, a new beer coaster. A few minutes later, after pushing my way past Spiderman and Thor on the increasingly busy Boulevard, another man of similar appearance approached and asked where I was from. As I told him, he looked excited and informed me that he'd just performed in Melbourne at the Big Day Out.

The first comedy club I attended in LA was the Laugh Factory on the Sunset Strip. While the Laugh Factory itself is a chain, this was its original and most famous venue. Its logo comprises a distinctive orange and yellow circle atop a sky-blue background, like a Hollywood sunset. It's the backdrop of many famous stand-up routines I'd seen on TV or YouTube over the years. This was also the room in which Michael Richards, who brilliantly played Kramer on *Seinfeld*, went on a bizarre and shocking racial tirade in 2006 when heckled by two black men. Richards was very apologetic in the aftermath, and it resulted in the banning of the word 'nigger' at all Laugh Factory venues, with comedians receiving a $20 pay cut every time they use it. The record fine issued since was $320 for Damon Wayans, himself a black comedian, who used it sixteen times in one set.

While it was great to experience such a famous venue in person, I walked away that night feeling a bit disappointed — not by the quality of comedians, but because all I remember hearing was racial humour. Followed by more racial humour. And more. And then a little bit more racial humour for good measure. Now, racial humour done properly and tastefully can be very funny, and most of it was done very well. But surely it doesn't have to be the *only* style of humour on show at one of the world's most famous clubs. It genuinely became quite tiresome. (In fairness, I was reliably told it's not always this way.)

However, to put this in perspective, I reminded myself this is a city that had massive race riots twenty years earlier following the Rodney King bashing and the subsequent acquittal of the police officers involved. As Australians I don't think we truly understand the concept of civil disturbance. By LA standards, these riots involved mass violence, destruction, looting, arson and murder. In the aftermath of the King verdict, sixty-three people were killed over six days of lawlessness and the US infantry was required to restore peace. Now, imagine that in Melbourne or Sydney. Most of these comedians would have been children or teenagers when that occurred. And the riots were not based on just one incident. Rather, they were the straw that broke the back of decades of underlying racial tensions, which are still far from resolved. If the best comedy was sourced from personal experience, then it stands to reason that racial humour is so prominent here. Perhaps LA was the prime example of how comedy, like all artforms, will reflect its society and can play an integral role in confronting social issues. If racial prejudice and hatred can be diffused by years of mockery, perhaps it begins to lose its power.

The next evening I made my American debut! I can't explain how exciting that was to post on Facebook. It felt like such a lifetime achievement, despite the obvious fact that *anybody* can fly to LA and put their name into an open mic ballot. Still, I happily claimed it as my first big step onto the international stage.

The basement bar at the Hollywood Hotel was labelled *The Bomb Shelter* when hosting its open mic comedy nights, in recognition that it's ok to bomb here. Despite its rather pessimistic moniker, *The Bomb Shelter* was a hilarious comedy room and I laughed more here than at the world famous Laugh Factory the night before. As there are usually a lot of comics vying for open mic time in LA, it's common to go into a ballot which doesn't guarantee a spot. On this night, however, there were about twenty of us, so we were told everyone would get on stage for five minutes and the ballot would merely determine the order.

As it turned out, my name was drawn well towards the end of the night, but surprisingly I wasn't that nervous as I sat watching the other acts for the first two hours. I'd like to think it's because I was well prepared, but it was more likely because I was so far from home that if I bombed badly nobody from my regular venues would hear about it. While the quality of acts was still hit-and-miss, there were plenty more hits than misses.

Noticeably, pretty much every amateur comedian seemed to be taking their craft very seriously, focusing on tightly written set-ups and strong punchlines. There was less rambling than I was used to in Melbourne.

I was beginning to notice something else about the open mic experience in general – it can be wonderfully sociable. Since first setting foot in LA, I'd been struck by an incredible sense of aloneness that I hadn't anticipated. It sounds bizarre to feel lonely in one of the world's biggest cities, but when you travel solo to the other side of the world and don't know anyone, the sense of feeling alone in a crowd can be quite overwhelming. More so than I'd anticipated. I'd travelled alone before, but had hung out with Australian friends in London, Paris and Switzerland, and a lot of our conversation had revolved around Aussie Rules and cricket. Here it was more daunting. However, I was discovering open mic comedy to be a great way to meet people and immerse in local culture. For starters, a lot of other comics are also there by themselves and happy to chat, and a genuine compliment on someone's set is normally a well-received conversation starter. On this night, for the first time, I felt truly comfortable in LA and enjoyed good, humorous conversations with many other comics. As usual I was often asked 'Where you from?' (I was often mistaken for British or, strangely from one bartender, South African) and I promised a few of my new friends a tour of the Melbourne comedy scene if they ever made it that far below the equator. For solo travellers – whether you're a comedian or not – I can recommend open mic nights as a great place to tuck in for an evening.

I'd been having such a great time, I almost forgot I was getting up on stage. By the time I was called to be 'on deck' (a baseball term for the next batter to the plate), the room was still almost as full as it had been at the start with about fifty people, meaning more than half the crowd were punters. When I was announced on stage by the MC I was thrilled by my walk-on theme *Down Under* by Men at Work, the unofficial national anthem of Australians overseas (only Aussies can understand how a song with a Vegemite sandwich reference can bring a tear to the eye). And at this point, I impulsively decided to exaggerate my accent. I've always been jealous of comedians with accents, so I must have figured this was a rare chance to get my own natural edge, and what appeared on stage was the most ocker version of myself I've ever met. Also unusually for me, my opening came rather spontaneously during a conversation with another comic just moments before stepping up. It's commonly advised to not change your routine at the last moment unless you're responding to something that's happened within the room, but it's a gamble I decided to take.

To set this up, what first time visitors to LA often don't realise is that Hollywood, as a district, is quite a downtrodden area. It has a tragic number of homeless people and a high crime rate. Many travel guides advise you not to stay in Hollywood, but it was only after booking a cheap hotel there that I realised this. The glitzy name is more of a concept. Today, Hollywood Boulevard is just a tourist attraction, and the movie stars live miles away in lofty Beverly Hills, Bel Air or Santa Monica. While I wish I'd known that earlier, it is through mistakes, I've noticed, that great comedy can appear.

'So anyway, I'm staying on Sunset Boulevard in West Hollywood...'

I tried to feign an expression that was somewhere between confused, ignorant and dumb out-of-towner, which by now came naturally.

'Do you know how good that shit sounds when you're booking online from the other side of the world?'

I was relieved when this got an instant big laugh, even some applause. It would have been awkward to open my set by insulting everyone in the room. But it landed reassuringly well and I moved straight into some cultural observations as a newcomer to America, such as their annoying refusal to adopt the metric system. 'I don't know inches and feet! Now I have to visualise everything by Subway sandwiches.' I even found humour in their culture of road rage, and recounted witnessing an assault on Highway 405. 'I don't want to be considered a hero at all, I just did what any of you good-natured Americans would do... I filmed it.'

I finished with a flourishing statement about how much I loved LA, which I was told would earn me a huge round of applause on its own. It did.

It was so much fun, I cancelled my plans to visit another venue the following night and went back to *The Bomb Shelter* for more. A few of the same faces were there but it was mostly a new crowd and I had another great night, meeting more local comedians and trying out some more new bits. I promised myself that if I ever returned to LA, I would definitely come back to this wonderful basement bar.

On my final night, I went to the HAHA Cafe in North Hollywood. They offered open mic spots from 6pm before the main show at 8pm. This was a much larger area, a professional comedy club more like the Comic's Lounge back home, but it felt incredibly empty with only about twenty people in it when the open mic started. By now I was getting used to the 'All the way from Australia...' introductions as I stepped up on stage and did about ten minutes – pretty much the same material

I'd done over the past two nights. It was a good experience to speak in front of 300 chairs, even if 280 of them were empty. I got a few laughs but nothing substantial, as the rest of the room was mostly other comedians scrutinising their own notes, and when some of them stepped up they were extremely impressive. More of a fun experience than a real gig, I was still content with my set and decided to stay for the main show. For my last night in LA, I figured I'd sat through enough open mic by now and it was time to witness more professionals firsthand.

I grabbed a drink and relaxed into my seat when, in a bizarre and unexpected moment, hundreds of people streamed in through the doors. It reminded me of the Boxing Day sales back home! Within minutes the place had gone from nearly empty to standing room only – from quiet and sparse to a cacophony of conversation. It seemed odd that so many people must have been made to wait outside merely for the sake of open mic, but I soon realised some of the acts I'd just seen were professionals practising their sets for later (which explained why they were so good). The instantly packed house also said a lot about the vibrancy of the LA comedy scene – that a club like this can fill so easily on an ordinary weeknight. By comparison, the Comic's Lounge will only sell out on the most popular nights. Comedy club culture still seemed a distinctly more American thing.

As I enjoyed watching the professionals, some for the second time that evening, I reflected upon what I'd learned from LA. Very clearly, the material of mine that had received the best laughs had been observational – my foreign perspectives of American culture. Despite what some back home had warned me, Americans so far were actually quite good at laughing at themselves, at least at the hands of an Australian. But more to the point, I felt it was my personal reaction, my subjectivity to the differences that had made the jokes work. In the same way that my material back home had begun to work better when I opened myself up on a personal level, I was beginning to perceive that the true subject of my best comedy was not what I was explicitly talking about. The true subject was *me*. For example, Hollywood being an undesirable neighbourhood in itself is not funny. That could be joked about in ways that may position the audience to feel sorry for those who live there. What made my opening line work was my personal reaction to it, my ignorance of local culture and my shock upon arrival. *I was always the true subject of my jokes.*

With renewed awareness of the importance of subjectivity, I would continue to observe it critically in the work of many skilled professionals, such as the ones on stage at the HAHA Cafe who were thankfully doing much more than just racial humour tonight.

During one of the breaks, I was approached by two lovely young comics, a man and a woman. We'd seen each other perform and chatted for a while about how I was enjoying LA. Then they told me they would be going to a few different clubs with some other comics over the next few nights and they were wondering if I'd like to join them. It was a genuine invitation for no other reason than they liked my act and wanted to welcome me into their group. I was so touched by this, and excited by potentially making real friends in LA. Who knows what could come of that? It was *eternally* frustrating that this was my last night there. I had a flight and hotel booked for San Francisco the next day, and a ticket to see my beloved Golden State Warriors in my first live NBA match. I still thought long and hard about the offer, but eventually, and painfully, declined. We enjoyed another drink and then parted, and I swore to myself that the next time I travel I will be much less organised.

There must be very few obese people in San Francisco, I thought, as I huffed my way up one of its many almost vertical streets. When you experience how hilly it is you wonder, jokingly, why anyone would have thought to build a city here. And when you read about how close it sits to the San Andreas Fault you wonder, in all seriousness, why anyone would have thought to build a city here. However, perhaps the beauty of the Bay Area is reason enough to take the chance.

On my second afternoon in San Fran, I went for a pleasant stroll across the Golden Gate Bridge. Strangely, despite sharing the bridge with thousands of other people, bikes and cars, it was a wonderfully tranquil experience and I spent a long time gazing at the azure San Francisco Bay and its myriad of sail boats. From such a height it was a truly majestic image. The bridge itself is an equally impressive sight. As the world's largest suspension bridge at its completion in 1937, it spans 1.7 miles (about 2.7 kms) and is listed as one of the Wonders of the Modern World. It is a quarter of a mile high and joins San Francisco to Marin County, with more than 100,000 cars passing over it per day. However, thanks to a documentary I had recently watched, the only statistic I could think about while standing on one of the world's most awe-inspiring structures was that on average one person per week jumps off the fucking thing.

I had learned this courtesy of a film called *The Bridge*, in which director Eric Steel spent months filming the Golden Gate Bridge in order to capture actual suicides (sounds like a real first date movie, doesn't it !). I stumbled across it on YouTube while researching San Francisco and, despite being horrified, I ended up watching the whole damn thing. In fairness, it is done tastefully and examines the lives of some of the victims, speaking to their families and only using the footage with their permission. Steel reportedly kept his promise of promptly calling police every time he observed somebody acting oddly. But, overall, it left a very unpleasant aftertaste for me. Seeing actual jumpers was too disturbing for a relatively mainstream release, in my opinion, and if there was one film I could erase from my memory, this would be it (although *Star Wars Episode 1: The Phantom Menace* might give it some competition).

As I contemplated this strange juxtaposition of beauty and death, I was not to know that in only a few months one of my comedy idols, and one of Frisco's favourite sons, who was credited with leading 'San Francisco's comedy renaissance' in the 1970s, would himself die by suicide. When Robin Williams was announced dead on August 11, 2014, the outpouring of grief was almost unprecedented in my lifetime. It demonstrated how close we can feel to those who make us feel good and laugh. Many people said they felt as though they knew him, even all the way from Australia. The Melbourne comedy scene went into mourning and many tributes flowed on social media from today's generation of comedians describing how much Robin had inspired them, even those who wouldn't be old enough to remember him pre-*Flubber*. It was eventually confirmed that he suffered from Lewy body dementia, a degenerative disease that devastated his brain, affecting its production of dopamine – the 'happy' chemical that effectively keeps us alive. In fact, there has been conjecture over whether this should even be classified as a suicide. Before understanding this, there was a lot of speculation in the media about his lifelong mental health, and it was wrongly suggested that he suffered from bipolar disorder, initiating public conversation about a perceived link between comedy and mental illness. There is a stereotype of comedians being tortured souls who tell jokes as an attempt to dispel their inner demons, the extroverted persona a mask for a more depressive one. Even though this was not the case for Robin, the reasoning was plausible given the adrenalised highs we all saw. While I'm sure all stereotypes, including this one, are based on an element of truth, I still consider this a gross exaggeration, as most comedians I know are attracted to stand-up merely as a popular, instant and fun form of creative expression. In fact, a lot of creative arts – including poetry and music – seem to carry the same stigma, as though sadness is the key to the purest creativity. I don't agree with that at all, as surely everyone feels sadness at some point in their lives. Some just use their creativity to navigate through it.

It was comforting to read that Robin's ashes were scattered in San Francisco Bay. Next time I'm in this beautiful city, gazing out at one of the world's most alluring bodies of water, I'm sure I will picture him cheekily grinning back.

My trip ended with a short stay in Las Vegas, which I soon realised would have been better with a partner for a romantic time, or else a bunch of mates to run amok at least ten years earlier. But I enjoyed my time there; I saw the Grand Canyon, played poker and blackjack for a handy return, and saw Jason Alexander – another *Seinfeld* actor – live on stage. What a fitting way to end a memorable trip, being in the same room as George Costanza!

While in America, I met many charming, welcoming people. I got the feeling Americans are like proud homeowners who enjoy showing off their house to visitors. For some reason, this defied my expectations. There were only a couple of people I really did not enjoy talking to. One of them, a woman perhaps in her late forties, was sitting near me at the Jason Alexander show. When it was established I was from Planet Australia, she was intrigued.

'So, you guys, like, drive on the wrong side of the road, right?'

'Well, no,' I corrected her, 'we drive on the *other* side of the road.' I thought this would clarify a misconception and we could start talking about kangaroos as usual, but no.

'No honey, you drive on the *wrooong* side of the road.' Then she turned to her friend. 'I don't know why they don't just make everyone drive on the right side of the road! That would make so much more sense.'

Ah, there it was, another endearing American trait – a myopia that results in their domestic baseball competition being called the World Series and the reason why the film *Deep Impact* features two comets hurtling towards Earth that are remarkably both predicted to land in the USA, one on the east coast and one on the west. (Mind you, if you surveyed the rest of the world, many people may not have a great problem with that.)

Thank you America, I had a truly wonderful time. I'd love to come back and see you again soon.

8

BUSINESS TIME

Upon returning to Melbourne I got back into the open mic scene, but as work commitments became tiring around the hard slog period leading into winter, it became much easier to stay home on cold, rainy nights than to battle inner city traffic, find a car park and sit through a lot of other amateur comedy just to do a five to seven minute spot. I didn't want to lose momentum, but during this period I probably averaged only one gig per two to three weeks, which is nothing if you're trying to advance. As much as I wanted to keep getting up on stage and moving forward, life was keeping me busy, so I took a break of sorts.

And at this point I'd like to take a slight tangent from my narrative…

As you've probably figured by now, at this stage of my life I was a single man. I'd never been married. I'd enjoyed some lovely relationships but none had gone the distance. And while I was more than comfortable with the single lifestyle, upon returning from America I decided it might be time to meet some new people.

I'd met a few good female friends through comedy, but most were either much younger than me or, by contrast, much older, divorced and using comedy to unleash fury upon the male of the species. Online dating was the obvious way to hook up these days and while I'd dabbled in it previously, I hadn't found much more than good comedy material. And to be honest, the online dating scene for me still lacked an element of fate. If I was ever to marry, I'd want to tell a truly unique and amusing meeting story at the reception (wedding audiences can be easy laughs). I'd like a story that was at least more interesting than 'we both swiped right'. For example, one of my best mates got to know his future wife when a playful food fight broke out at a pub and she threw a nacho across the room that landed in his drink. At the time, Brad was upset about guacamole in his beer, but I ended up telling that story at his wedding. I'd love to have a similar tale myself.

I decided upon a compromise of sorts – speed dating. This is a live event in which participants can meet twelve to fifteen potential partners and 'date' them for six minutes at a time. It combines the traditional fun of meeting in real life with the economy of meeting many people at once. It sounded like a good fit. If anything, it was time efficient, because if it didn't go well I could at least condense a whole year's worth of bad dates into just one night with a free glass of champagne.

As it happened, Teddy and another good mate Jay had recently tried their luck with one of Melbourne's leading speed dating companies. They'd had an okay time, but didn't meet anyone of interest and had found the event a little stilted. Nevertheless, I took the plunge and signed up with the same company for an event the following week in the trendy inner suburb of Prahran.

Wearing a neat shirt and slacks and the rare scent of cologne, I arrived early and purchased a drink on the ground floor. The speed dating function was upstairs, and I had some time to get my thoughts together before stepping up. I had a couple of butterflies, but generally felt pretty relaxed (one of the benefits of stand-up is it conditions you to nervousness – speed dating and almost everything else now seemed easy by comparison). While waiting, I began to think about what I could talk about with my dozen or so dates. I hadn't really prepared any mental notes for conversation, which was starting to feel like a mistake. From my usual experience of dates, the first six minutes can be the most awkward until you hopefully settle into a free-flowing conversation and the rest of the night can be more relaxed and fun. What I was about to experience was the most awkward part of the date a dozen or so times over. Suddenly six minutes felt like a long time to fill!

And as I contemplated this, an incredibly unfortunate coincidence then occurred.

Now, dear reader, this is the bit where my story may become a bit hard to believe. Especially as comedians rarely let a pesky little thing like the truth get in the way of a good anecdote. But I reiterate that *everything* in this book is completely true. That is essential to me. For better or worse, my life requires no hyperbole. What happened next, I guarantee you, *actually happened*. As I sat waiting to go upstairs, I looked up from my drink to see probably the last sight you'd ever want to see before a speed dating event: my most recent ex-girlfriend!

Generally I've managed to stay on good, friendly terms with former partners, but this time things were more awkward than usual and I really didn't want to see her again. And even if I had wanted to see her, this would be the *last* place I'd want to see her. My only saving grace was that I'm pretty sure she didn't notice me as she walked through the bar and straight up to the speed dating room.

I couldn't believe my eyes! Of all the nights! I continued to stare at my half-drained pint for what must have seemed like a ridiculous time and swore under my breath until the beer turned warm. Sadly, I drove home without even making an appearance upstairs. While I'm sure this may seem like a real waste to some of you, it just wasn't worth it for me to reopen this particular door. I'd rather just forfeit my money and come back another time. I stopped by Teddy's front porch, the site of many past contemplative beers, and lamented that my speed dating night had been even less fruitful than his, given that his had at least started.

A few days later I emailed the company to apologise for my absence and, rather ambitiously, enquired about redeeming the cost of my ticket for a future event (perhaps there was an ex-partner clause?). I wasn't expecting a positive response, but their reply still shocked me:

'No.'

That was it. No greeting, no explanation. Just 'No'. And two hours later came a follow-up email:

'In fact, failure to turn up results in a six month ban.'

It was that blunt. And what especially perturbed me was the two hour follow-up, as though they had been stewing on it.

My initial shock soon turned to outrage at the rudeness of the company and the indignity of being banned. *Banned!* Who gets banned from a speed dating company? I agreed it made perfect sense to not issue a refund – just like any event, if you purchase a ticket and don't show up it's your loss – but the ban was clearly over the top, and the hostility of the response indicated very poor customer service. And this was supposedly one of Melbourne's leading speed dating businesses.

A few things festered in my mind over the coming days. While I was seething over being banned, I was also thinking about how much untapped potential the speed dating market suddenly seemed to have in Melbourne. If one of its leading companies was so rude and unprofessional in their customer relations, and if the events were considered rather awkward and stilted, perhaps there was room for something different – something much more casual and friendly with an emphasis on laughter. Perhaps these events even called for... comedians?

I've always had a keen interest in small business. I've enjoyed spotting gaps in the market, just for a bit of fun and hypothetical conversations with like-minded friends. And this one was emerging, I must admit, as one of my favourites. A comedy show interspersed with rounds of speed dating – it seemed like such an obvious combination! The more I thought about it, the more I felt like the person who first thought to add tonic to gin.

For the first time I actually began to consider *starting* a business rather than just leaving it in the space of another vague, unfulfilled idea. Was this something I could actually do? Not to replace my teaching job of course, but perhaps a little earner on the side? I was currently paying a mortgage by myself, so a second income, while not essential, would be extremely handy.

From a marketing point of view, I understood the competition for such a business would not necessarily be other speed dating companies – so I couldn't take much comfort from their shortcomings – but rather the Goliath that is the online dating world. However, I had a sense that the time was right for a shift in the marketplace. I was only speculating of course, but people in their late twenties had by now grown up as the 'Tinder generation', and it stands to reason that those who haven't found love by swiping may now be looking for other options. Was there an emerging demand for more real-life meeting experiences? Was the natural order of society swinging back towards more real-life settings? If so, perhaps my idea would be exactly what people were looking for. The best social lubricant by far is laughter.

The idea began to solidify in my mind. I could aim to run one event per week with potential to expand if it became popular. Importantly, I wasn't driven solely by the prospect of extra income, but also by how much fun it could be. And it would give me a chance to regularly perform comedy on my own stage. I would not be the main comedian, rather the 'warm up' guy to an employed professional, so I could practise interacting with audiences while still leaving the main laughs to somebody more accomplished. I proposed the idea to many people, both business-minded mentors and single friends who represented my main target market. Overwhelmingly, all gave a similar review – this idea was so good, why had it never been done before?

I decided to do it! Until recently, I never thought I'd have the conviction to go through with starting a small business. But then again, until recently, I never thought I'd have the courage to perform stand-up comedy, especially in LA. Goals, I was learning, can be achievable for those willing to have a crack. That afternoon I registered the business name COMEDY SPEED DATING.

How hard could it be?

Well, as it turns out, it can be really bloody hard. The process of establishing a small business would normally be rigorous at the best of times, but when you have a slightly unusual product you can add several more layers of red tape. I learned a lot about stuff that I won't bore you with, but as an example, even identifying this type of business was difficult. In online documents there is never a 'speed dating' or even 'dating service' option in drop down boxes, so unless you can specify 'other', you need to find the closest thing. To this day there is a record of me at a major bank as the owner of an 'introductions/escort service'.

While dealing with website development, booking system software and marketing, I must admit I had doubts about my ability to get this project off the ground. I believed in the idea and desperately wanted to see it work, but on top of my busy job and everything else in my life it was already becoming a burden. And I was trying to do it as cheaply as possible, which in hindsight is a mistake for any business, despite how easy it may seem from the outset. The concept had felt like such an epiphany at first, but perhaps it was time to return it to the status of great potential business ideas that never see daylight.

At around the same time, another coincidence occurred. This time it was a much happier one.

Andrew invited me to a birthday party for Darrin, a mutual friend who I hadn't seen in years, so I gladly went along. Miscalculating his age for forty, I turned up expecting a huge do and a great catch-up with old buddies, only to realise he was forty-one and the only other person at his BBQ, apart from his family, and Andrew and myself, was his new next-door neighbour Sarah.

Sarah and I hit it off straight away. She was another teacher, with a former life in tax accountancy (she'd had an epiphany of her own), and worked at a specialist school for disengaged teenagers – one of the toughest gigs in education. That takes much more courage than stand-up, and I was soon to learn she was brilliant at her job. She took great interest in my comedy and was intrigued by my business idea.

The following week we caught up for a first date, and thankfully it lasted more than six minutes. She cooked a scrumptious lamb roast and we dined al fresco in her backyard with red wine, and a candle that served the dual purpose of keeping mozzies away. We spoke a lot about Iceland – a country she had lived in for a couple of years as an exchange student and a place I'd always longed to see. Sarah was to become my new partner in more ways than one; we were about to enjoy many wonderful times together, and she also inspired me to persevere with my speed dating idea, keen to share the adventure as an unofficial business partner. It probably wouldn't have been possible to start up without her motivation and business experience, and I am extremely grateful for all of it. Outside of our new relationship, Sarah's enthusiasm, hard work and useful contacts saw Comedy Speed Dating get off the ground within a few weeks. Even though the business was registered in my name, it very much became ours. And, moving forward, her support of my comedy in general was also to become invaluable.

The inaugural Comedy Speed Dating event took place in early 2015 in the function room of a traditional South Melbourne pub. Thankfully, we'd discovered that venues were often fine to waive a fee for use of function rooms on weeknights given we were bringing thirty or so patrons who would spend on food and drinks. That gave us great footing to make a profit, as our only major expense was to hire a polished comedian.

The first guy we employed did an okay job. Just okay. Admittedly, it was our first event and we were experimenting with formats. But more to the point, I think we set him up with a difficult gig. This was a good lesson for me in understanding comedy audiences, as perhaps I'd been naive to presume that if jokes are funny enough, people will just laugh. In reality, it doesn't work like that. Positioning an audience to laugh depends on many factors, such as physical space. Small spaces with people sitting closely together enables laughter to be more contagious, unlike in our large room with tables spaced farther apart for ease of conversation. And a major factor, of course, is the audience's emotive state. Our customers were turning up mainly for the dating, not the comedy, and they were probably feeling a bit anxious. Most of them are not getting half-drunk with friends beforehand and settling in for a big night of laughs. Instead, many will turn up alone, feeling self-conscious and probably keeping an eye out for ex-partners (imagine that!). The comedian did alright with what we provided him. But overall, the two comedy segments at the beginning of the event and after the interval were a bit flat. I'd created a tough gig, so admittedly it was on me. But I also felt he was looking for an easy job with rehearsed material, and what we really needed was somebody to embrace the challenge and interact a lot more with our crowd.

Our second event was one week later in the function room of a more modern pub in Richmond. This time I paid more attention to the setting, placing tables closer together, and ensuring groups of friends were seated closely if possible. We dimmed the lights and placed candles on each table, creating an intimate environment more conducive to romance – and hopefully laughter. We had a few more patrons this time, with fifteen male and female tickets sold. For our first event, I'd been forced to bring in some single male friends to make up the numbers. And while they were happy to get free tickets, and genuinely trying to meet women, it was a strategy I hoped would not be necessary for long. An interesting trend I noticed from the outset was that women were signing up faster than men. I had anticipated the opposite.

All we needed now was a comedian with great crowd skills to work the room. The whole evening – in fact, the entire early reputation of our business – depended on it. These days it doesn't take long for bad reviews to spread online, and even for our own confidence we needed this night to go swimmingly. We engaged a talent agency, and their recommendation was Tom Siegert. I hadn't seen Tom before, but some of his YouTube clips were hilarious and he'd performed at the Comic's Lounge plenty of times. However, I was a bit unsure about his rather laidback style. Would it translate well to a speed dating environment? Time would tell. When Tom turned up he greeted us enthusiastically and immediately checked the lighting and his positioning in the room, and tested the microphone. He immediately struck me as a true professional. I don't think I filled him with confidence when I explained this was only our second event and we didn't really know what it was all about yet. But he seemed to embrace the challenge.

As guests arrived, most people seemed relatively relaxed and happy to mingle before the event started. Sarah was magnificent at greeting people and making them feel at ease. We provided nametags and colourful folders with scorecards, on which guests could mark 'yes' or 'no' next to each date's name so I could then organise the matches and send contact details the next day. Sarah had a great eye for detail too, adding plenty of adornments and extra candles throughout the venue. This event was already feeling as though it had a more positive vibe, but I was a bit concerned when two of our male guests had not arrived by starting time. I phoned them both, getting no answer from one, and another told me he'd changed his mind and couldn't really be bothered coming in tonight. He even asked if he could just come to the next one, presumably to redeem the cost of his ticket. I was quietly fuming, but remembered that I'd done a similar thing to another business recently, so in a measured tone I explained it doesn't work like that as we require even numbers to make events work. A gender imbalance will leave gaps in the dating, and inevitably one group will feel unsatisfied. I encouraged him to purchase a ticket for another event (which was at least better than *banning* him).

Fortunately, to help keep guests occupied and socialised we had some extra help. Recently I'd been emailed by a woman in her twenties named Leah. She'd identified herself as an actor between jobs and offered her services in any way we saw fit. She didn't specify any role or suggest a price, she just liked the idea and thought it would be fun to be involved. I appreciated her direct approach. She was enthusiastic, so I thought it couldn't hurt to get her in for at least some early events to help out while we were finding our feet. She could mingle with guests, talk to anyone who looked alone, and provide table service while the dates are running. When Leah arrived, Sarah and I provided her with one of our new Comedy Speed Dating T-shirts and we looked, for the first time, like a truly professional team.

As guests were happily mingling, I let the pre-drinks last a bit longer – a good move because by the time we seated them they appeared more relaxed and sociable than at our previous event. I opened the show with a few jokes about single life – one advantage of this audience is you know they all have this in common – and some of the pitfalls of online dating, which worked well. By a stroke of luck, one guy's phone went off as I was in-between jokes. He hurriedly silenced it, and I held a mock phone to my ear and said, 'Sorry honey, I'll be home tomorrow'. That got the biggest laugh so far, and even I was mildly impressed, as spontaneity had not been my strength to date. The audience was nicely warmed up as I introduced Tom.

Tom Siegert began with some strong material that immediately had the audience laughing as one. This was *exactly* what we wanted. He then interacted with a few with great effect. I'd given him a vague instruction to talk to the audience without putting anyone down or making anyone feel uncomfortable. Looking back, I've got no idea how any lesser comedian would have handled such a briefing, but Tom was a natural. Leah and Sarah sat in the seats of the two guys who hadn't shown up so the women at the tables wouldn't feel uncomfortable. But for some reason there was still one gap. Tom investigated and found a nametag.

'Where's Toby?' he asked.

A voice from the back of the room piped up. Toby had been running late and was scoffing a quick chicken parma before the dating started. A brief conversation escalated into a bit of good-natured banter before Toby hurled a decent attempt at a heckle, but Tom batted it away like Don Bradman: 'Well that's a great way to start fifteen dates, mate – show them all your passive aggressive side!' That one floored me as well as most of the guests.

As I rang the bell for the start of the dating, the feeling in the room was exciting and I could tell everyone was engaged and enjoying themselves. The comedy had helped people to relax and make easier conversation. This was exactly the way I had pictured it months ago.

I was glad to see Leah chatting to people who may have been alone at any time. It was important that people could have a positive experience that could be measured in more ways than simply whether they ended up naked with someone who had been a stranger four hours earlier. Soon, I was surprised when a guest asked me discreetly whether Leah was from a popular drama series on network television.

'I don't know,' I replied. I didn't watch much commercial TV. When someone else asked the same question, I suddenly wished I'd read Leah's resume more carefully. As it turned out, Leah De Niese had recently portrayed a lead character in *House Husbands* on Channel Nine. I suddenly felt guilty that I'd employed somebody relatively famous, dressed her, and asked her to serve drinks for a modest cash payment. But to be fair, she seemed to love it. It's not just a stereotype that actors spend a lot of time out of work, and this was a fun and unique way for her to fill some gaps in her schedule. She happily came back for a few more events until she landed another TV role. After that, Sarah and I would enjoy spotting Leah in various shows and commercials. It became a bit of a game.

As Sarah and I stood back and watched the fun unfold, I was struck with an overwhelming feeling that *I did this*. None of these people would be here now, having all this fun, if I'd never had this crazy idea. It was quite a bizarre feeling, as though the part of my brain responsible for impulsive and potentially embarrassing ideas had had the curtain yanked back, exposing it to the world. I'd taken a chance and it was paying off. I'm so glad I did.

It was a similar feeling to getting up on the comedy stage.

'If you've had a good time tonight, folks, please make sure you tell all your friends, like us on the socials, spread the word to all your single mates,' said Tom at the end of the evening, closing the show to a loud and enthusiastic round of applause.

'And if you didn't have a good time tonight… Um, well just shut the fuck up really…'

Later that night, as Sarah and I enjoyed a few drinks in the main bar with a group of daters who had remained to hear the band and continue chatting and laughing, I was beaming with pride. Our second event had been an overwhelming success and we finally realised what our product was.

Hopefully, nobody was going to need to shut the fuck up.

9

LOVE AND LOLS

The next few Comedy Speed Dating events went pleasingly well. We were attracting new customers who were having a great time, often hanging around afterwards and continuing to socialise until the venues closed. It was incredibly fun to run and I was feeling more like a party host than business owner at times. Tom Siegert was continually successful, and on one occasion he asked to bring a friend – a fellow comedian who was interested in doing some material.

'He's a bit different,' explained Tom, 'but I think he'd be a good fit for you.' Tom offered to sub him out of his own payment so, backing Tom's judgment, I said yes. The more comedians we could get the better. And it was especially helpful when comedians mingled with guests, which Tom was good at, so it would be great to have more hands on deck. Don Tran turned up the following week.

Don was an emerging comedian of Vietnamese background. He was quietly spoken as I welcomed him and explained how happy I was for his offer, and that it would be wonderful if he could socialise with guests, just to make some general conversation and ensure nobody felt left out. He nodded without saying a lot, and as guests began arriving and mingling to the background of my subtly themed playlist (including *Get Lucky* by Daft Punk and the theme song from *Fifty Shades of Grey*), Don remained sitting in a corner of the function room. Fair enough, I thought, it was his first speed dating performance and he actually looked quite nervous. As I took to the microphone to commence the show, I noticed he was looking even more squirmish.

'Is he ok?' I whispered to Tom. 'If he really doesn't want to do this he doesn't have to!'

'He's alright,' Tom reassured. 'I told you, he's a bit different.'

As Don eventually stepped up to the microphone, he looked out at the guests as though he had just woken up and didn't know where he was. And without acknowledging the crowd or even smiling, he launched into one of the funniest routines I've ever heard. His depressive state had all been part of his persona. Don Tran is a deadpan comic, a Vietnamese Elliot Goblet. His whole act was a string of unrelated one-liners that were funny in their own right, but with such straight-faced delivery he had me and most of the guests in tears. I can't remember most of his lines despite laughing so hard at them, but one that I can't stop visualising is: 'I wonder if Kevin Rudd has ever referred to his genitals as the stimulus package.'

It was probably the funniest night we had, and Don didn't smile once.

I was pleased to see plenty of people achieving matches and couples beginning to form. It was an extremely satisfying reward. And I was continually overwhelmed by Sarah's devotion to the business. Her tireless efforts in helping with the time consuming things, such as preparing nametags and scorecards, and calling customers before each event to confirm bookings and reassure their nerves by answering questions, was invaluable. She really seemed to enjoy it. She even managed to source a couple of ridiculously cheap billboards through a contact she had in the industry. It seemed big companies were moving away from traditional poster-style billboards in favour of the even more intrusive electronic ones, so bargains were to be found. Our first one appeared outside Clifton Hill train station on busy Hoddle Street. To passing motorists, Sarah and I must have looked odd posing for photos in front of a billboard, but the sight of our company logo with the by-line 'Find some love and LOLs' emblazoned so publicly filled us both with immense pride. It was not the most romantic spot for such a message (in fact, a couple of years later I saw the exact site used for a recreation of the Hoddle Street massacre of 1987), but it got our company name out there. Even better was to come, with our second billboard on platform one of the very busy South Yarra train station.

Tom soon became occupied with his growing family, as well as the development of his hilariously satirical character the Suburban Footballer who was to appear on the AFL *Footy Show*. To replace him, he recommended another friend of his, a comedian he described as one of the best up-and-comers in Melbourne.

'I reckon he's perfect for you, mate. Have you heard of Evan Hocking?' he asked over the phone. The name sounded familiar, but I couldn't quite place the face. 'His brother plays for Essendon,' Tom added, as though that would clarify things. As I was sitting at my laptop, I quickly Googled his name and immediately recognised Evan as the sporty guy with reddish hair who I'd met at my third gig at Station 59.

'Oh yes,' I said emphatically. 'He'd be great.'

'Cool, well he's recently gone pro and I reckon he'd be keen. I'll see if he's interested and send you his number.'

I thanked Tom sincerely and was relieved when Evan told me he was enthusiastic for the role. Evan's first event was in Hawthorn and he was fantastic – engaging the crowd and getting them laughing from the beginning, and mingling with people all night.

The main quality that makes Evan such a great comedian is his likeability. His persona is one of those knockabout 'blokey blokes' that everyone would love to have a beer with, however I'm not sure if that even qualifies as a persona as it's actually just who he is. It's always refreshing to hear comedians get great laughs by being positive and not putting others down or making anyone in the audience feel uncomfortable. The derogatory, and at times dark, styles of comedy that pervade the open mic scene don't normally progress much further than small niche markets. Conversely, Evan has what it takes to be widely popular, even famous one day.

On Evan's first night, I have forever been disappointed in myself for ringing the bell straight after the break to draw attention to his second set, only for people to misinterpret it as the beginning of the next date and launch into their conversations. I hesitated, and within seconds it got to a point where interrupting them now would have been unpopular and a poor way to reintroduce a comedian, so I let them go, denying Evan half of his material. But I'm a big believer in always *learning* from mistakes rather than rueing them – a philosophy I instil in my students, and myself in business, comedy and life.

While I was thrilled with the quality of comedians we'd been lucky enough to attract so far, I still had one concern – they'd all been male. At events where there is a natural gender balance, I thought it might be good to mix it up with the performers as well.

One night at Hawthorn as I was signing in guests, I greeted a woman who identified herself as Mimi.

'Mimi?' I repeated, panicking slightly as I scrolled through my list, unable to find her name. Sarah and I were both meticulous in double-checking all bookings, but I was beginning to think we'd finally made an embarrassing oversight.

'Did you book online?' I asked, stalling for time.

'My friend booked for me,' she explained. 'It was a thirtieth birthday present.'

'Happy birthday!' I offered, while frantically shuffling paperwork. For such an emergency I had prepared spare name tags based on the most common names, but I was sure Mimi would not be one of them.

'She might have booked under Amy,' she added. 'Amy Shaheen.'

'Oh, thank goodness,' I said, with a deep sigh of relief. 'Yes, we have a booking for Amy Shaheen. Is that not your correct name?'

'That's fine, it's my legal name. But I never use it, everybody calls me Mimi.'

Throughout the night, I noticed Mimi having a good discussion with Evan, and by the end she approached me and enquired about the opportunity to try a comedy spot with us the following week. She'd never performed comedy before, but had always wanted to give it a go. She'd written some material and was looking for a friendly place to start. I was initially a bit reluctant, as it was important for our business image to have polished comedians only, but the timing could not have been better for her as I was keen for a female comedian to share some duties with Evan. Her idea was to do a five-minute spot, and she did not want to be paid. If she was any good, this could be just what we were looking for. And to be honest, I thought back to my own first gig – two years ago now at Station 59 – and how intimidating it was. If I could offer an aspiring comedian a step up into a brave new world, then I'd be happy to do so.

What we saw the following week was a first gig that impressed me more than any I'd witnessed before. Firstly, Mimi had a way of not appearing nervous – a ridiculous skill that I will probably never master – and proceeded to get good laughs from the entire audience, particularly women. This was perfect, I thought. While Evan got plenty of laughs with his blokey style, Mimi complemented him perfectly by speaking directly to the women in the audience who could relate to her dating dilemmas. In one anecdote she described how her friends were meeting hot guys through their work and were wondering why she couldn't do the same.

'That's fine for you,' she'd reply. 'You're a hairdresser – you're gently massaging their scalps for a living. I'm a social worker!' I can't remember the exact wording of her 'Barry from Doveton' punchline, but it absolutely killed.

I ended up slipping her a small cash payment as a token of our appreciation and an incentive to return, and we were very grateful that she did so frequently. And to this day, I'm sure Mimi Shaheen is one of the very few comedians who can boast about being paid for their first gig. For our next few events we went with the Evan and Mimi double act and it worked like a dream.

At one stage I received an intriguing request from the Austereo network. One of their Melbourne radio stations, KIIS FM, was having a promotion called the *KIIS n'Tell Hotel*, which involved getting a bunch of young singles together and basically locking them in a hotel for a night with plenty of booze and reporting on shenanigans the following day. It sounded like a radio version of *Big Brother*. I was asked if I'd like to be involved as a 'socialiser'. To be honest, I had no idea what that meant, and I don't think they did either.

'What exactly do you want me to do?'

'Just introduce the singles at the start of the night, have some fun, play some games, you know – just whatever you normally do.'

'What do you think actually happens at our events?' I felt like saying, but didn't. I had no idea what they expected of me, but the event was part of the *Hughesy & Kate* drive time show, so I was just thrilled to be asked. It could be a lot of fun and some wonderful free promotion. So a few days later I turned up to the ritzy Como Hotel in South Yarra, where a temporary radio studio had been set up on the rooftop, alongside a cocktail pool party.

Dave Hughes is one of the most popular and successful Australian comedians of all time. I'd seen plenty of his live performances over many years and have always admired him for getting the absolute best out of himself. His story of being on the dole in Warrnambool as a kid without much direction in life became the staple routine of his early days. I remember watching his first appearance on *Hey Hey it's Saturday* in the mid 90's and thinking he was hilarious despite looking extremely nervous (he's since admitted it was the most nervous he's ever been). Since then, his distinctive drawl has become one of the most widely recognised voices on Australian TV and radio. And despite his highly strung and slightly dazed persona, he is very intellectual with an astute business brain. When I first shook hands with him at the Como, he was straight-faced and businesslike – completely at odds with the voice I'd heard just moments earlier as he wrapped up a live broadcast. As I explained my business venture and what I was considering doing for their event, he thanked me and told me he would give the business a mention on tomorrow's show.

I was then taken to a room to meet the contestants, a bunch of good-looking young extroverts who had successfully auditioned to be here. For speed dating events, Sarah and I had come up with questions for daters to generate some fun conversations, so I used these as the basis of a getting-to-know you activity:

'What's your favourite part of the body and why?'

'If there was a movie about your life, who would be best to play you?'

'If you woke up as the opposite gender, what's the first thing you would do?'

The conversations were recorded with some surprisingly funny and quirky results. I could feel the ice breaking.

Once the party started, I was asked to roam with a microphone and speak to a few of the guests, mainly enquiring about who they had their eyes on and what budding romances they could see developing. This was part of a pre-record for tomorrow's show, and I knew only a tiny bit would be used on air – if anything – but as I mingled and spoke to as many guests as I could, getting some amusing grabs at times, I contemplated how extraordinary it was to find myself here on the Como rooftop, holding a microphone at a KIIS FM party, mingling with Dave Hughes and Kate Langbroek and about thirty hot young singles, and having a great time. I was reminded of the extraordinary places you can find yourself by following through with your 'crazy' ideas.

Soon I was thanked by a producer and invited to relax and enjoy the rest of the party. At one point I had a good chat with Hughesy, firstly about my speed dating business. He was quite interested, especially when I told him I offered paid spots for comedians, so if he knew of any (of course he knew hundreds) who were looking to earn some cash they could get in touch. Then the conversation turned to footy and we rated the chances of his beloved Carlton Blues against my Tigers in an upcoming match. The Blues were pretty lowly at the time and he reiterated how having a good sense of humour can be vital as a football supporter.

The next afternoon, Sarah and I sat glued to KIIS FM from 4-6pm. In between the music and ads, the whole show was devoted to the *KIIS n' Tell Hotel*. I don't recall hearing any of the audio I recorded, as most of it was from that morning as the contestants recalled their exploits, and having met them all it was genuinely fascinating for me to hear the juicy gossip that Sarah only rolled her eyes at. By the end of the show we were still waiting for Comedy Speed Dating to be mentioned and thanked. They were leaving it quite late, I thought, and by the time the show finished we were mortified that we had not been mentioned at all. Not once!

I was outraged. I had worked hard last night, volunteering hours of my time, and I'd been told informally by a producer that my business would receive an on-air mention – a message reiterated by no less than Hughesy himself. By now I was just feeling exploited. And to top it off, Sarah and I had just spent two hours listening to the Pussycat Dolls and Justin Bieber. I was about to write a strongly worded email along the lines of

'You can KIIS my arse!', but Sarah wisely talked me out of it. Instead, I rang the producers the next day and explained my disappointment. To their credit, they couldn't have been more apologetic, and a few days later I was completely blown away when the event featured in the Gossip section of the *Herald Sun*, Melbourne's most widely read newspaper. Beside a prominent picture of Hughesy was a short article that concluded with '... *the event was hosted in conjunction with Comedy Speed Dating*' with our company name bolded. This was a major win, as a plug like that in the *Herald Sun* was worth more than a brief mention on radio, especially as our most important target market at present, males over thirty, was not a significant target audience of KIIS FM, despite the comic genius of Dave Hughes.

About two months later, Austereo made another request – this time to repeat my service for an event run by Gold FM, a popular 'golden oldies' station. This was much more within our demographic. They were running a *Family Wingman* event, in which singles were invited to bring along one family member to act as their 'wing' to give their approval or otherwise of potential matches. This time my briefing was even more vague, but I turned up to the popular Wellington Hotel in Flinders Street looking forward to another fun night. It was part of the *Jo & Lehmo* breakfast show, and I was greeted by well-known radio personality Jo Stanley, who was extremely courteous. Lehmo, another popular comic who appears on a lot of TV and radio, was good fun as well. It's funny how when meeting someone relatively famous it can feel weird for a few seconds, but then you're just speaking to any other person. Again, I spoke a bit of sport – the universal language – with Lehmo.

There were probably thirty to forty singles this time, all lucky listeners who had phoned in to win their spot, so with their wing-people it was a much bigger crowd. They were singles of all ages, from eighteen to over sixty. I offered to do the same sort of introductory activities as last time, or some new ice-breaker games I'd been thinking of, but the producers preferred me to simply roam and talk to people, encouraging them to feel comfortable. Doing so, I got to know as many guests as possible and I began to introduce people who sounded compatible. I had a great time, and also managed to hand out plenty of business cards to the singles and even a few of their wings. In the end I hope I added some value to the evening, as it was genuinely fun and I was thrilled the next morning to not only hear our company name promoted by Jo and Lehmo, but I was personally thanked as well.

Lehmo: 'And we must also thank Ben from Comedy Speed Dating.'

Jo: 'Ben did a wonderful job… helping people to mingle and have some laughs, which is really not an easy thing to do…'

I remember the wording precisely because we used the audio for one of our social media promotions. I was thrilled for the business to be getting more widely publicised, especially through free opportunities that we never could have anticipated.

For our final speed dating event of 2015, we had a Christmas special and I self-indulged by performing all of the comedy myself. I felt like I was ready to sustain the entire night, and I was pleased with my performance. After getting Sarah to introduce me on the microphone (which, quite frankly, was like getting a cat to take a bath), I managed to work the room well enough, I believe, to give people value for money. In fact, a great benefit of running the business so far had been that it was a wonderful opportunity for me to practise crowd work – one of the toughest comedic skills. While I had performed less open mic in this time, the experience of running Comedy Speed Dating had been just as good, maybe even better, for my development.

Over Christmas we took a break. I went to a friend's wedding in the charming Irish city of Galway, and then achieved another bucket list item by visiting Iceland, where I met up with Sarah as she proudly showed me around this awe-inspiring country. By luck, the stunning Northern Lights were out on our first night. On the way, some friends and I spent a few nights in London and I took the opportunity to perform open mic in a small basement bar. It was a fun spot, but I was just happy to say I'd now performed comedy in three continents!

Resuming in 2016, selling enough tickets to turn a profit was still challenging. Despite a run of great promotional opportunities, our database of interested clients was not expanding by much. The problem was still mainly with men. Plenty of women were keenly signing up, but men were becoming very difficult to attract. I paid for a series of live reads on sports radio station SEN to speak directly to a mostly male demographic, but it barely made a difference. On one occasion, former AFL footballer David Schwarz read the script as though he was trying not to laugh. We ran some early events but then decided to take a short break. Unfortunately, it became a permanent one as we never quite found the drive to get back into it with the gusto required to make the business work.

As much fun as Comedy Speed Dating had been, running a business while working busy jobs was becoming quite draining for both Sarah and me. Perhaps the venture could have worked if we'd committed more time and money to it, but in the end it was always supposed to be a side business – just a bit of fun. What I hadn't anticipated were the many, many hours we'd spend trying to sell tickets, communicating with clients, dealing with venues and attending to so many tedious administrative tasks, which really negated the fun in the long term.

I was fascinated by the fact that men were so much harder to sell to than women. I knew from many wasted years in nightclubs that men will distinctly outnumber women in any setting that can potentially lead to sex. That was just a fact of life, never questioned. Why then did speed dating seem to be the opposite? I had some theories. Firstly, I could observe how women seemed to greatly appreciate the element of control that speed dating provides. Several women commented that when they're out in a bar and guys are hitting on them, they'd often give anything for a bell to ring forcing them to move on after six minutes. Conversely, I think many men resented that loss of control. They didn't like the pressure of the shot clock, as Evan noted. And from chatting to blokes, I figured many have become too accustomed to dating apps where you can scroll through hundreds of women's profiles, rejecting most at a cursory glance. Who would want to waste six minutes talking to someone these days? I'd originally thought there might have been a swing back towards real-life meeting experiences, and I still believe there will be, but we weren't seeing it in time for our business to flourish. Also, Tom astutely observed that women like to glean as much information as possible from a man before dating him, so a setting akin to a job interview suited them well, as opposed to a dingy nightclub where blokes will happily veil their true selves behind dark lights and alcohol. I was learning a lot about the species.

In the end the business didn't work as planned, but it was certainly worth the effort. Even though it never endured as a long-term venture, it still provided me the brief but gratifying experience of running a small business, another lifelong ambition, along with a unique way of developing my comedy skills. Quite often on the customer feedback sheets we'd see comments such as 'This is so much better than [the original rude pricks who banned me]', which always made me chuckle. We'd done a good job overall. Most of all, Sarah and I had experienced some incredibly fun nights with the satisfaction of knowing we'd created them ourselves, and for us it had been a wonderful bonding experience in our new relationship. Also, we'd met some inspiring people, including Tom, Evan and Mimi, who we became good friends with moving forward.

While I never maintained any system for following up on couples that had matched through Comedy Speed Dating, I know that two personal friends of mine, who I had invited for free to make up the male numbers, are still in loving relationships with the women they met. That fills me with tremendous pride, and I know there must be plenty of similar stories out there. Much later, I received an email from a lady who thanked me immensely and told me she was expecting her first child from her current partner, whom she'd met through Comedy Speed Dating. It is stupefying for me to consider there is by now at least one life in this world that exists only because I decided to follow through with a 'crazy' idea. For everything that child achieves as it grows up, for every life it touches and for every future person descended from that child, it all happened because my ex-girlfriend walked past me one night in

Prahran, leading to me getting banned from a speed dating company and spitefully beginning my own.

That.

Blows.

My.

Mind.

Also, Evan made a couple of appearances on the AFL *Footy Show* just a few months before it was axed after twenty-five years on television. He only takes it a little bit personally.

10

THE LOUNGE

'We're all fucked up, insecure individuals,' observed John Burgos.

John is a professional comedian and actor, and this evening I learned to my delight that he played the Annoying Devil on the Australian version of *Balls of Steel* – a hidden-camera prank show in which he would be wonderfully annoying to unsuspecting members of the public while dressed in a bright red devil costume. A typical day for the Annoying Devil might involve playing a trumpet next to people speaking on their phones, dumping live eels into a public swimming pool, or projecting a giant penis onto Sydney Harbour Bridge. (I often wondered how the career advisors at school would react if a student aspired to this, as John is living proof that one should never completely rule out such a dream.) At first I had no idea that I was in the presence of one of the stars of a show I'd enjoyed watching and discussing with mates. I respectfully informed John that the Devil wasn't our favourite character, as we also appreciated the work of the Nude Twins – two blonde ladies who disrobe in public eliciting shocked and awkward reactions from bystanders – but John reminded me that the twins were new to series two, and he had been on the show long enough to work alongside Katia Taylor, the original Nude Girl. We shared a moment of misty-eyed reflection, and then got back to the reason why we were at The Comic's Lounge.

Located in Errol Street, North Melbourne, the 'Lounge' was currently Melbourne's most popular professional comedy club, and every Tuesday it hosted an evening specifically for professionals to try out new material. While the events were ticketed like any other and crowds could sometimes be quite large, people attended knowing they were effectively watching comedians workshopping. Despite this, nights were still always lots of fun and rarely felt like anything less than a polished gig. Before these shows, the Lounge would run a workshop for aspiring comedians overseen by the professional MC of the evening. They weren't structured lessons, rather a chance for us to present a few minutes of material on stage and receive feedback from the professional and others in attendance. During the most productive workshops, we could see material evolve from something potentially funny to bits that were tightly written and well delivered. It was a wonderful opportunity to improve some of my own bits, however even if time didn't allow me a chance to perform every week, as the workshops were normally well attended, it could be just as valuable to observe and participate in the group discussions. Sometimes the workshops would run much like my favourite classes to teach, ones that generate passionate discussion and feedback from many students. And it felt great to be a student again.

The workshops also gave us a chance to perform on the same stage as some of the world's most famous comedians, as long as 'stage' is taken quite literally as the woodwork beneath our feet. Sometimes *really* big international names would perform unannounced at the Lounge, particularly before major tours or festivals, which would delight the punters on the night. Even the best comedians in the world need to workshop their material somewhere, and a good piece of advice for comedy fans is never leave before the headline act if it's advertised as a 'surprise guest'. I once did a workshop just days after Chris Rock performed a surprise gig on the same spot in the lead up to his *Total Blackout* arena tour. To stand on the same performance space and handle the same microphone as the guy who had hosted the Academy Awards a year earlier felt surreal.

Apart from John Burgos, during this period I had the chance to workshop material and listen to advice from many others, including Jeff Green, Khaled Khalafalla, Johnny Kats, Doug Chappel, Michael Chamberlin and even old mate Tom Siegert. For just $10 this represented exceptional value to any aspiring comic, especially considering we were allowed to stay and watch the main show afterwards. And excitingly, some of the regular attendees could be offered a five-minute spot in the show, among professionals performing in front of a real, paying audience. The spot had to be earned and the material sharp, but this was a golden opportunity for amateur comics to experience their first professional stage time. I was seeing several of the more accomplished open mic comedians finding their feet, literally and figuratively, on the big stage on Tuesday nights at the Comic's Lounge. From early on this became a short-term goal of mine.

The workshops were barely advertised but for word of mouth among the comedy community. I found out about them though Mimi. Her own passion for comedy was growing exponentially, and she was already becoming well ensconced in the scene. It was good to begin catching up with her on most Tuesdays.

'We're all fucked up,' repeated John to the group of about twenty of us. 'We all have massive insecurities in life. Your audience does too.' He was talking about the way in which many comedians joke about their insecurities, and audiences laugh not to be cruel, but predominantly because they can relate to them. John discussed this in response to a new bit I presented.

To set this up, recently I'd overheard a conversation in which two staff members at my school had been discussing the merits of pay TV service Foxtel. One of them suggested it was overpriced, and the only program he regularly enjoyed was American reality show *Hardcore Pawn*. Now, clearly in Australia we don't use the word 'pawn' unless playing chess. Aussies will instead 'hock' their second-hand goods or just dump them onto their neighbours' hard rubbish, so the pun within this show's title can potentially be misunderstood. On this occasion, it led to an awkward moment that was quickly rectified with a laugh, before the conversation went back to whinging about report writing and how long until the next school holidays as usual.

This staffroom banter on its own was clearly not enough to be funny, but here was a *premise* for a potential routine. I was learning that the more you look out for them, the more you can find good premises almost anywhere. I jotted this one down and began brainstorming ways to make it funny.

At first I wrote an anecdote in which I was chatting to a female friend about *Hardcore Pawn* and she misunderstood the pun. The first laugh was based around my initial embarrassment and the awkward pause in which she began to contemplate me as a fan of the heavy breathing channels. But the twist and punchline was her revelation that 'It's ok, I enjoy a bit of the hard stuff myself.' I even had her list some of her favourite titles. I ran this at a Lounge workshop, but it didn't quite hit as well as I'd hoped.

'It's good, but I think you're the one who needs to be the most embarrassed,' was a comment from one comedian. She was right, the awkwardness had to be felt by me as the narrator. I had to position myself to be the victim.

'Does it really sound like a big problem to have?' asked another comedian, getting a bigger laugh from the group than I did for the bit. John agreed, and recommended that I try some variants that expose my insecurities more. I had to be more vulnerable in the story.

Driving home from North Melbourne that night, my head was brimming with how comedy can have so much to do with basic human psychology. In particular, why do we get so much pleasure from others putting themselves in embarrassing situations? Why has laughing at the misfortune of other people been such an age-old source of hilarity? We even have a name for it – 'Schadenfreude' – which comes from the German words for harm and joy. In comedy's earliest days, pies in the face and people falling over was gold. Even chimps have been shown to react to such silliness! How primal is this instinct? Could it be that we are projecting our own insecurities onto others? If it's true that we are all fucked up on some level, is it comforting to know that other people are as well?

Eventually, the anecdote became one of me bringing a date to my parents' house for dinner. I'm nervous about impressing my new partner, and proud of the fact that so far nothing has gone wrong. During the dinner conversation, my partner lists *Hardcore Pawn* as one of the shows she enjoys, and the usual misunderstanding causes a moment of awkwardness. But just before I can explain the pun, my father pipes up in an effort to save any embarrassment and admits that he and my mother don't mind a bit of the hardcore stuff themselves. This version began to get a good, reliable laugh. (And needless to say this anecdote is entirely fictional, not a family secret, just to save any further confusion!)

Overall, the workshops became a great way to focus on the craft of writing. It was increasingly clear that good material doesn't just appear, it often goes through an extensive writing process. And writing, I was learning, means much more than driving to a beach house with an exercise book and beers. Writing in a comedy context means experimenting with different forms and structures of a joke or routine and running it in front of audiences until it works reliably. A strategy I picked up from the Lounge was to record every set on my phone and listen back to it, analysing not so much my own performance but, more importantly, the audience. Don't listen to yourself, comedians would recommend, listen to the laughs. Audience reaction is the only true gauge of good comedy writing.

It's commonly agreed that professional comedians need to write about one hour of new material every year in order to stay fresh and innovative. When I'd first heard that many years ago, I'd found it hard to believe – one hour didn't sound like much at all, particularly for professionals. But now that I was seeing how much work can go into just a few minutes of new material, it made sense. One hour of professional quality material is a huge body of work for a year. That's why it is important for professionals to have opportunities such as the new material night at the Lounge, and to make surprise appearances on smaller stages. That's where they do their writing.

In a way, I was taking some comfort from observing how much writing actually takes place behind the scenes and how intensively some material is workshopped. Good writing, not spontaneity, was emerging as the most important skill of a successful comedian. To the outsider, the opposite appears true. This suited me, as writing was definitely my greater strength.

It was encouraging to watch Mimi get stage time at the Lounge on Tuesday nights. She was rapidly developing as a comedian, and to see her name projected on the background screen in the manner of the professionals was inspiring. It reinforced my short-term goal of seeing my name on the same screen.

While I was content with the way my material was developing, lately I also felt as though it was lacking overall cohesion. I seemed to be developing bits about random topics that were getting good laughs on their own, but overall I wanted fewer jokes and more routines. When on stage, I carried a cue card in my back pocket in case I ever forgot what I was planning to talk about (thankfully to this point I'd never needed it) and it might read something like this:

CRICKET

SOBER

HARDCORE PAWN

NEW PHONE

PENGUINS

GEORGE PELL

ONLINE DATING

JESUS TOAST

(I've often wondered what people might think if I ever lost my cue card and it was found outside of a comedy venue.)

While each of these bits may have been working well individually, I really needed something to tie them together. I wanted more routines in the true sense of the word, not simply a bunch of jokes that could be easily interchanged if forgotten. Watching the big festival galas, where the world's best comedians will present a tight five minutes, they will never do a bunch of unrelated jokes, they will do one sharp routine.

Plus, writing longer material would be an easier way to allow more of myself to come through in my comedy. I'd already begun steering my writing towards subjective views and experiences, now I really needed to explore who I was on the stage. For example, a joke about people who camp out in shopping centres for a new phone can be funny in its own right. But it can be even funnier as part of an overarching routine about society's increasing dependence on technology. Add to that the narrative perspective of someone struggling to keep up and feeling cynical towards those obsessed with their devices, and you've got not only a funny routine but an emotionally open narrator who the audience can now empathise with. I needed more of this.

I liked my *Hardcore Pawn* bit and wondered if it was possible to develop it into something longer, maybe as part of a routine about the tribulations of finding love. I had other material I could tie in with that, especially jokes left over from the speed dating nights, but at this stage I didn't feel like focusing too much on that topic. By now it felt a bit cliche and, quite frankly, I was over it. And I now had a lovely new partner who probably didn't enjoy listening to my dating stories, even if most of them weren't true.

The moment it all came together for me was one night when I was chatting to Paul Sharplin – another relatively new comedian who, at the age of fifty-three, had started around the same time as me. Paul is one of my most admired amateur comedians. He worked hard on the open mic scene and had already achieved stage time on Tuesday night at the Lounge. I was a massive fan of his work. He bore a slight resemblance to George W. Bush, and comedy had finally given him a reason to be happy about this as he'd developed a wonderful routine about it. Paul gets along well with pretty much all other comedians, even those less than half his age. We could relate to each other as relatively old newbies to the scene.

He expressed to me one night that he liked my *Hardcore Pawn* bit, but reminded me I was telling the story more like someone in their twenties. He offered me a very important piece of advice that has shaped a lot of my writing since:

'Always remember who the audience sees on the stage.'

He was absolutely right, and it occurred to me how so much advice in comedy can be quite basic yet so profound. When I tell a story about bringing a date home to meet my porn-addicted parents, people aren't visualising a young bloke at the beginning of a new relationship, they're seeing a forty-something year old English teacher with slightly greying hair who is too old to be having these ridiculous moments. Even though a lot of comedic anecdotes may be fictional, they still need to be plausible. Audiences *want* to believe them.

I agreed this bit still needed some work and wondered whether it would it be worth my time to persist with it or just let it go. When unsure, sometimes it's good to pull a joke apart and start from whatever makes it potentially funny in the first place. At its core, the main laugh in this joke was actually not based on a gratuitous porn reference, it was based on me finding myself in a painfully awkward situation. While the porn punchline might have seemed a bit unrealistic, the prospect of finding myself in an embarrassing moment, in a general sense, certainly was not. So maybe it wasn't so unbelievable after all. In fact, did young people believe embarrassing situations simply stop happening after a certain age? At twenty, do we just believe that by forty we are too old and mature to make dicks of ourselves? Was there a humorous new angle here for me to explore?

It was at this moment that something finally clicked and several pieces fell neatly together. Almost overnight I wrote the material that would see me through for about the next year of comedy, my 'socially awkward' routine.

The premise of the routine was my inability to grow out of the awkward phase of life, with a broader message that we can't just presume it happens automatically as we get more candles on the birthday cake. By exposing a lot of my own vulnerabilities, I was inviting audiences to laugh at theirs. 'We're all fucked up insecure individuals,' echoed the voice of John Burgos in my head like the ghost of Obi Wan Kenobi.

I could more logically include a revision of my *Hardcore Pawn* bit here, as it now had realistic context. A bunch of other anecdotes fell seamlessly into place as well. Some were bits I'd been trying out, and some were just scribbles in my notebook. At first they were unrelated, but with the common thread of social awkwardness they began to gel nicely.

One was inspired from a time I was caught talking to myself in the car. Driving to comedy gigs I often rehearse out loud, which can sometimes be a problem when stopped at traffic lights. Once in Richmond I was overheard by a group of young women at a tram stop, so in an effort to not look crazy I pretended to be talking on my phone. I used this as a premise, to the point where it became a story about me being spotted by the police who mistakenly tried to book me for talking on my phone while driving. To get out of a ticket I had to plead the truth and convince them I was a stand-up comedian practising a routine. They asked me to tell them a joke with a funny punchline as evidence. I ended up with a ticket.

Another bit I'd been thinking about finally saw some light within the context of this routine. I'd first jotted down the premise when I'd heard a comedian in LA discuss receiving oral sex from a vegan. So far I'd tried to steer away from overly crass material, however I'd found this to be at least an interesting idea. His direction with the joke and punchline had felt a bit lazy and I thought I could turn the premise into a better joke. To date this had been hard to do without being gratuitously lewd, but through the lens of social awkwardness came a new perspective on the whole story. The humour was now based on my awkward killing of a romantic mood:

> 'I once ruined a really hot date by asking a socially awkward question. You see, we were out for dinner and I realised she was a vegan. Now, I don't know a lot about veganism, but a question popped into my head. Believe me, this is the sort of question that you would only ever think about when on a date with a vegan.
>
> I asked, "So do vegans... swallow?" [There's normally a short pause here before some knowing laughter.]

"Because when you think about it that's kind of an animal product." [This is my favourite part of the story and always gets a good laugh, but it's not enough to finish on.]

Turns out she'd never thought about that before… until she got back to my place later on.

And in the end, it was one of the dumbest things I've ever done. Because let's face it fellas, it's hard enough to get a blowjob in this world… without stopping to ask [dumb voice] "Does this meet your dietary requirements?'" [*Always* a big laugh here.]

I've since been proud that this bit evolved from a crass oral sex reference into something more contextual. It's commonly said that you should finish your set with your biggest laugh, and for a while this became my closer. Audiences loved it. And the socially awkward material became my first true routine that was long enough to sustain a full five to seven minute set. As it developed, it continued to get big laughs from a pleasingly wide range of crowds. Which was just as well, because soon I was offered my first spot at what was, after Station 59, my favourite open mic comedy venue of all. In my view, it was one of the best in Melbourne. I was very keen to impress.

11

TURBO CHARGED

In a typical working week, Monday is certainly not a preferable night to go out. Thursday is normally fine, and Wednesday has proven to be ok as it's over the hump. Even Tuesday can be manageable if necessary. But Monday couldn't be further from the weekend. However, days of the week barely seem to matter in the comedy community, and one of the many attractions of the show running every second Monday at The Brunswick Hotel was its ten dollar jugs of beer.

Funny at the Brunny was one of the best and most popular open mic nights on the Melbourne scene. It had a professional stage with flashing lights, a pumping sound system and DJ to get the audience energised, and on some nights it was hard to move through the crowd. Importantly, people were there to watch the show, so there was no competing for the attention of the audience or speaking to the fraction that were listening. It was a great gig, and booking a spot could take weeks.

It was run by Glen Zen, a hilarious comedian with long grey hair who was one of those inspiring middle-aged blokes who clearly wasn't ready to stop partying on weeknights. Glen is truly one of the nicest people I have met in comedy, and like Kieran Butler, he doesn't discriminate and is willing to give a spot to anyone who supports his room. *Funny at the Brunny* seemed to have a higher proportion of established or professional comedians doing spots, but others, including first-timers, were welcome among them. As a spectator I'd never witnessed a flat night, and before my maiden performance at the *Brunny*, I discovered that Glen gives a football style pump-up before each show.

'Benny, out here mate,' he beckoned after giving the crowd a five-minute warning.

I joined Glen and the rest of the comedians in the beer garden. He gave us the running order and I was to be sixth up – a good spot. No pressure to open the show, but not too long to wait. Glen said a few inspiring words along the lines of 'bring your best' and 'have a lot of fun up there tonight', and then we all did the thing where we put our hands together and raised them as a team. I loved this build up. Glen ensured we had the mindset of a group working together to entertain the crowd. It's so much better than other venues where comedians will stroll in just in time for their spot and leave immediately after it. Glen doesn't seem to tolerate that. At the Brunny it was team players only.

I was more nervous than usual for my first gig at this venue, but I was learning the art of channelling nervousness into excitement. I'd discovered a simple technique of changing the language of my inner voice. When it told me 'I'm nervous', I simply changed it to 'I'm excited', and repeated that to myself. It's amazing how something so simple could work so well. Again, it wouldn't work for the drug mule at an airport, but the whole point of comedy in the first place is to have fun. That's why I was there, and so was the audience. There is truly no other reason for comedy nights to exist. So I reiterated to myself that I should be genuinely excited every time I step up.

By now I felt pretty confident in my material, as I'd been doing the 'socially awkward' routine around town for a couple of months and it was becoming quite polished. I was getting strong laughs in regular places and for the first time I began to experience a kind of auto-pilot on stage, remembering material more instinctively without needing to concentrate as deeply. I took this as a good thing, a similar state actors often achieve when reading lines. However, I knew a trap to avoid was putting up a 'fourth wall' – an imaginary barrier between myself and the audience. This is an important difference between comedy and acting, as with comedy you always need to be 'in the room' and prepared to interact. Nevertheless, it felt good to finally have a solid five to seven minutes that didn't need much alteration so I could focus mostly on its delivery.

I found Sarah in the crowd as I waited for my spot. She was excited by this venue and asked if I'd like my performance filmed, as she'd done a couple of times before. While this was tempting, I told her not to worry about it. I truly wanted Sarah to just enjoy the show. Comics will often film each other as a favour, and I knew from experience that it can sometimes be tricky to make a good video (as someone with a big head will inevitably be standing in front of you, and the loudest talker in the audience will *always* be right next to the camera), which can detract from your enjoyment of the act. Sarah's moral support at so many of my gigs was invaluable, and on this special night I wanted to entertain her more than anyone else.

'Good luck,' she said with a kiss as I made my way to the side of the stage before my call up. 'Have you got your prop?' she added.

'Yep, right here,' I replied. 'Thanks again for making that.'

I should mention at this point that I was planning to add one more anecdote to my routine tonight. While I was originally hesitant to try a new bit at such an important gig, I rationalised that I would only do so if I was getting good laughs. I had confidence in the new bit, so I figured I might as well try it in front of a good crowd. The plan was that if laughs were flowing, I'd add it straight after Vegan Blowjob. If it didn't work I could still just use the old 'Sorry that's the first time I've done that bit and probably the last' gag, but hopefully that wouldn't be necessary. And for this new bit I required something I'd never used before – a prop! Sarah had artfully created it for me the night before and it now sat in my back pocket.

The lights dazzled and music pumped as the act before me thanked the crowd and the DJ called me up. The audience was having a great time and cheered me on stage, and bizarrely I bounded up the three steps with the pizzazz of Freddie Mercury. Thankfully, my opening line got a good laugh and my punchlines continued to hit well. In fact, before long I began to hear the cherished 'waves' of laughter of a large crowd laughing in unison. And like a surfer, it's on top of big waves that comedians get their true rush. For the first time I became conscious of it while up there. At most other gigs, I probably hadn't genuinely enjoyed myself until my set was over, but tonight I was aware of enjoying the pure experience of being on stage. Like never before, I didn't want to get off. Perhaps this night I discovered what is most enjoyable about being a comedian. Maybe these golden minutes in the spotlight are the trade-off for all the hard work that goes before.

As I concluded Vegan Blowjob, I had even the pool players at the back of the venue paying attention and laughing. That was the biggest endorsement of all. So I decided it was time to pull out my new bit.

To set this up, my new anecdote was a religious bit. As a staunch atheist I've never had a problem with religious humour, and I'd done some before. I don't like to offend people, but to me that's outweighed by the importance of free speech in comedy. Plus, I'm guessing any religious person spending Monday night in a pub is probably not that devout. I wouldn't do religious jokes at a church fundraiser, but at the Brunswick Hotel it's a free-for-all.

I explained that I was about to tell a story of probably the most socially awkward situation I've ever known. It occurred a few years ago when I'd been living with a mate called Pete, a born again Christian. 'Now, I'm not knocking anyone's religious beliefs,' I clarified, 'but what really shits me is the double standards some supposedly devout people live by.' Then I described how Pete would preach about God all week, and insist that my soul needed to be saved, but come Friday night he'd normally be out drinking. Saturday night he would often back it up with more. Then on Sunday he would stumble hungover into church and simply repent it all. 'Apparently it's that easy – that's all it takes!'

(I should point out that my story was fictitious, but certainly inspired by people I've known.)

'I'd say to him, "Pete, that's not very Christian-like, mate", and his reply would always be the same… "God was testing me. It was a test of my faith and I failed".'

Throughout this anecdote people laughed well, which was encouraging as they were clearly engaged.

'"Get your hand off it, Pete," I'd say. "That's not a test of faith. I'll give you a test of faith…"'

I continued by describing how one night the following week I cooked him dinner and slipped in a secret ingredient. And this is where my new prop entered the scene; from my pocket, I withdrew a small cardboard box painted to look like generic brand pills with TURBO LAX clearly printed on its side.

'Turbo Lax! Just like the shit from *Dumb and Dumber*! Who remembers that? There are some classic scenes in movie history, folks, like Robin Williams "Oh Captain! My Captain", or Leonardo "I'm the king of the world!"... But for me, nothing beats the scene in *Dumb and Dumber* where Jeff Daniels almost destroys the toilet.'

The audience was coming with me on this. I explained how sure enough, about five minutes after dinner, Pete ran to the bathroom holding his butt cheeks together with his hands. 'But what he didn't realise was that I'd snuck in earlier and removed every bit of toilet paper. In fact, the only bit of paper in that whole room was a small book I'd placed behind the bowl. Who can guess what that was?'

'The Bible!' someone reliably called out.

'That's right – the Bible!' Then I built to a crescendo: 'There's your test of faith my friend! Will you save your soul or your pants?'

As the climax of the story, this got the biggest laugh of all – big enough to close on. I thanked the crowd to great applause and felt ecstatic that the new bit had worked so well within a set I had already been thrilled with. I'd turned my nerves into excitement, delivered polished material and thrown in a new bit with confidence. It felt like my best performance to date, and Sarah agreed it was the best of my gigs she'd seen so far. I knew I still had a long way to go to be on the same level as many of the more accomplished comedians, but I felt as though I'd taken a big step tonight. I'd performed in LA and London, but it was here in Brunswick on a Monday night that I began to feel as though I could actually become good at this if I kept applying myself. And I'd finally discovered how to enjoy comedy in the moment – perhaps the most important step of all.

While happy with the way my material was developing, I did need to consider the irony that when I first started comedy I'd vowed to be clean. Apart from Seinfeld, I was significantly inspired by the likes of Adam Hills, as intellectual and observational humour has always been much funnier to me than the smut and dick jokes that can be reliably heard at comedy venues small or large. But here I was, with my best routines to date covering hardcore porn, oral sex with a vegan, and tricking a Christian into almost shitting his pants.

How far had I strayed from my vision? Despite the fact I was getting laughs, was this the comedian I truly wanted to be? Had I taken an easier path? I raised this at a Tuesday night workshop at the Lounge.

'It's a matter of establishing your own style and persona and being consistent with it,' advised the very popular Doug Chappel. Other comedians agreed, and one added, 'Did you know Jerry Seinfeld has never sworn in a routine?' I was amazed to consider that. I'd seen Seinfeld do copious routines (some of his best work is not on the TV show), yet I couldn't recall him swearing once. It would have seemed so removed from his clean image. I had at first modelled myself on him, and yet sworn like a trooper. So convincing is Jerry's persona I can't even imagine him swearing in real life, whereas people who didn't know me would by now presume I could barely get through breakfast without cussing at my toast. Perhaps I had to pay more attention to establishing a style and persona and staying consistent to it, resisting the urge for easy laughs at the expense of image. I had to establish who I was on the stage. Seinfeld is clean-cut. Hughesy is often angry. Elliot Goblet is deadpan. Vince Sorrenti is exuberant. Adam Hills is Mr Nice Guy. Judith Lucy is cynical. Jim Jefferies is half-drunk and opinionated. What was I? It felt like I was still just a guy telling jokes, and anything could come out of my mouth. This is another reason why comedy is about *so much* more than just writing good material.

For the next couple of weeks I decided to experiment with a few different styles. If anyone had been following me they might have thought I'd been knocked on the head, as I was clean-cut one night, semi-drunk the next, and I even tried being deadpan once but from me it just sounded ridiculous. I was no Wright, Goblet or Tran.

'That was deliberate?' one barman said with a great sense of relief. 'I thought you were having a stroke!'

Eventually I decided not to overreach. Surely my true persona would not be too far away from who I am, as I still wanted to play myself on stage, not a character. As long as I was consistent and remembered who the audience was seeing, as Paul Sharplin had wisely advised, I could let my persona evolve. It's commonly suggested this doesn't happen overnight, which was reassuring, but importantly I became conscious of it moving forward.

One Tuesday the workshop was hosted by Steve Hughes, a comedian whose persona is unmistakable. Known as the 'heavy metal humourist', his Wikipedia page states the best job title

I've ever heard: 'Thrash metal drummer, comedian and actor'. If you've never seen Steve Hughes, I can assure you the picture you already have in your mind is very close to what he really looks like. He often enters the stage to riffs of Slayer or Motorhead, and his social commentary can be just as brutal. None of us performed this evening, we just enjoyed an hour of Q and A time with Steve in front of the largest turnout for a Tuesday I had seen.

'Comedy can be a tough gig,' he explained when asked about his transition from the music scene. 'At least when you're in a shit band you're not the only one on the stage.' He spoke about how it took him a few years to find his voice in comedy, and I was relieved to hear this from a seasoned professional. Perhaps my own journey was tracking quite normally after all. He is now one of Australia's most popular voices for edgy comedy, which he describes as the 'funnest' type, but reminds us that for social commentary 'you really have to give a fuck'.

Steve divulged his thoughts on the concept of offensive material, a topic he is quite passionate about. He has a popular routine in which he mocks grown adults who moan about being so terribly offended by a comedy routine. 'So what?' he replies. 'Be offended. Nothing happens! You're an adult, grow up and deal with it.' As unsympathetic as that may sound, he doesn't mean it in an uncaring way. He doesn't *want* anyone to feel offended, he just doesn't care if people are. To me, that sounded like the perfect attitude for a comedian. He explained to us that 'being offended is subjective, it has everything to do with you as an individual and your moral conditioning. What offends me may not offend you. I'm offended when I see boy bands for god's sake!' We all laughed at that one. 'If you believe in free speech, you've got to be prepared to listen to some shit.'

He finished by talking about a fascinating topic, one that I hadn't given enough thought to previously.

'Learn how to use silence,' he instructed. After watching him MC the Lounge later that night, I noticed that he did use a lot of it effectively. It wasn't the type of silence that's often heard on the open mic stage when the performer has forgotten what to talk about. It was strategic silence, for effect. It's exactly the same pausing I recommend for my students when performing their oral presentations, but for some reason I'd never embraced its use in my own act. If anything, I am guilty of jumping too quickly from one idea to the next. I had no idea why I did that, however Steve explained immediately.

'Some comics like to fill the air with talk because they're scared of silence. It gives the audience a chance to *get* them. But to be silent is to hold your guard.' This was profound advice and I vowed to practise using silence more effectively. It was amazing how in comedy even saying *nothing* can be a challenge.

If I was to be honest, I *was* terrified of giving the audience a chance to jump in. I loathed unexpected conversation on stage and wished I could always just follow a script. The fourth wall was my friend. But I knew audience interaction is an unavoidable comedic skill and, while I'd gotten better at it through Comedy Speed Dating, I still needed to learn much more about it.

Comedians on big TV specials generally have very little interaction with the audience, but in most comedy venues it is much more common. In fact, the smaller the gig the more important crowd work can become. Sometimes it can be the funniest part of an act. Good comedians can turn to crowd work when their material isn't going well, and I've seen it used to re-engage noisy or inattentive groups and bring them back into the show. Crowd work can also be a very effective opening for a set, or a segue between different subjects, reminding the audience that you're in the room and the fourth wall doesn't exist. As much as I'd like to develop my crowd work, the fear of it not being funny, or even worse an audience member being funnier than me, was still a daunting prospect.

By chance, this was raised in a workshop a couple of weeks later and I learnt a lovely new oxymoron: 'practised spontaneity'. As it turns out, conversations on stage that seem spontaneous can actually have a lot of predetermined writing behind them. If you ask a question that is closed-ended, in that it requires only a brief answer, there can be only so many responses a person can give. Clever retorts can be stockpiled. Of course, crowd work won't always go to plan and there is often a place for genuine spontaneity, but stockpiling responses can, at times, work extremely well. This was told to me by a very well-known comedian. As he MC'd the Lounge later that night I paid particular attention to his crowd work and he did, indeed, have some great lines in response to audience interaction. Some of them got huge laughs, as audiences love quick-witted comebacks, but the next time I saw him on TV I heard the exact same 'spontaneity' floor the audience again. It's actually quite brilliant. I'm not going to name this comedian because to do so would be like giving away someone's magic tricks. But this technique is common and effective, so in the same manner I endeavoured to write some audience questions into my routines.

Another night, the workshop was hosted by Khaled Khalafalla – a younger comic who was extremely accomplished. I recognised him immediately as the opening act from Jim Jefferies' recent tour. Sarah and I had gone to the stadium show that set a record at the time for the biggest audience ever to specifically attend a comedy gig in Australia (over 6000 people). As the opening act, that made Khaled the first person to perform to a crowd of that size. I could not, for one minute, imagine what it would be like to perform in front of that many people, but he looked ridiculously relaxed. And when I've seen him perform at the Lounge he often sits, folding his legs up on the seat like a teenager at school having a casual chat. I would give anything for that confidence.

Khaled went around the group and asked what we were trying to achieve from our comedy – a question I'd been thinking about lately without a clear answer.

'Just to keep having fun,' I told him when it was my turn, 'and maybe one day to be in the pink magazine.' I was referring to the latest guide to the 2017 Melbourne International Comedy Festival that had just been distributed with the *Herald Sun*.

'Yeah? When do you think you'll do that?'

'I don't know, one of these days.'

'One of these days? Why not next year?' Khaled said matter-of-factly.

He had a point. Of the hundreds of acts advertised in this year's guide, a decent proportion of them were semi-professionals or amateurs just like me. Several of them I knew personally. While the prospect of doing a festival show had always felt like a distant dream, perhaps it was now closer than it seemed. I'd been performing and studying comedy for over three years by now, which is nothing compared to most others, but I was beginning to feel as though putting on my own show was something I could realistically aim for. Perhaps the next time someone asked what I was trying to achieve with my comedy, I could have a more definite response.

Sadly, the Comic's Lounge soon ceased to run the Tuesday workshops. No formal explanation was ever given. It was rumoured that the amateurs who appeared on stage, bringing their best five minutes, were sometimes upstaging the professionals trying new material, however I don't think that was the case. It's remained a mystery of sorts, and I've missed those Tuesday nights. As comedy is really the only artform that necessitates being practised in front of an audience, the regular opportunities to give and receive feedback had been invaluable, as was the chance to interact with accomplished comedians and to meet plenty of others on the same journey as me. I was disappointed that my short-term goal of performing to a paying audience at the Lounge had to be put on hold.

But my conversation with Khaled had reminded me of my initial conversation with my hairdresser Rose years earlier. Why *was* I waiting to put on a festival show? Why not aim for next year? Without making a solid commitment to myself just yet, I did allow the seed to be planted. In order to move forward with my comedy, an exciting new goal was probably what I needed. And I had to avoid forming any new comfort zones.

Seriously, how hard could it be?

12

RAW

Are you funnier than George? was the Wednesday night comedy show at George's Bar in Fitzroy. The bar had a Seinfeld theme and was effectively a shrine to George Costanza, so I was immediately in my element. Seinfeld paraphernalia was everywhere, from framed Yankees uniforms to Snickers bars served with cutlery. The venue mostly favoured experienced or professional comedians, however there were always two spots available to up-and-comers as part of their ongoing competition. At the end of the evening the audience would vote for who they preferred between the two newbies, and the winner would progress to the next round. While not a fan of competition comedy, and being vocal to friends and family about it, I did of course contradict myself by continuing to turn up and compete. I was pleased to make it through to the grand final in two series, but I never won overall. It was a bit difficult when at least one of the grand finalists would invariably turn up with twenty people to vote and I was there with only Sarah. Most of my friends had, by now, realised that to see me perform was to commit to a long night of hit-and-miss comedy, and I'd stopped testing friendships in this way long ago. Despite this, for my second grand final I did manage to attract a crowd of eight people from work, only to realise I'd invited them in the wrong week. In fairness, the temporary host from my heat had told me to come back on this date, but it worked out better anyway as after some last-minute messaging I managed to secure a replacement spot at *Stand up in the Attik* in Chapel Street, Prahran. While this highly regarded venue favoured accomplished comedians only, the incentive of bringing eight audience members can work as great currency, I discovered, and a fun night was had by all. By good fortune, Evan Hocking was on the same bill and it was great to share a stage with him again.

My first taste of real competition comedy was in 2017 when I first entered RAW Comedy – the official amateur competition of the Melbourne International Comedy Festival. The winner receives a cash prize and a fully paid trip to perform in Edinburgh, but for me the main incentive was to perform in the grand final show at the Melbourne Town Hall, televised on SBS. To qualify for such a huge TV gig, win or lose, would be the ultimate experience for this stage of my journey, so I wanted to give it my best shot.

RAW is a reputable competition for several reasons. Firstly, it's judged by industry experts, not the audience, so it's based on craft rather than who brings the most mates. Also, it's open to anybody, excluding professionals, to enter a maximum of three times. It has helped to launch the careers of many well-known Australian comedians, including Hannah Gadsby, Luke McGregor, Celia Pacquola, Ronny Cheing, Anne Edmonds, Sam Simmons, Adam Rozenbachs and even comedy statesman Lawrence Mooney. Khaled Khalafalla was a runner-up in 2011, just five years before opening for Jim Jefferies. There are many spots available across many heats held in great venues preceding the comedy festival, and the heats themselves can be a great experience in front of enthusiastic and relatively safe audiences (you'd have to be very unlucky to get heckled at RAW). The downside for me, however, was my age. It was generally accepted that judges were looking to unearth young talent. This is common knowledge without being officially stated, and grand final shows of recent years would rarely feature anyone much older than twenty-five. Last year there had been a finalist in her fifties, which kept some hope alive for me, but I knew that spots for relative oldies were rare and perhaps a little tokenistic. The previous year I'd watched a couple of great new comedians over forty deliver brilliant sets in a heat that had the whole crowd at Fitzroy's Evelyn Hotel in hysterics, yet they didn't even get voted through to the next round. I'd thought their sets were tight and worthy of progression. One of them actually asked the judges for an explanation, only to be told he wasn't allowed to do so, as judges weren't there to give feedback. With this realisation, the grand final spots for someone my age had perhaps dwindled from twelve to one. However, to once again draw upon Jim Carrey's character from *Dumb and Dumber*, I could hear a little voice saying, 'So you're telling me there's a chance!'

At first I didn't realise that the earlier you submit your application for RAW, the greater your chance to secure one of the most popular venues, such as the iconic Gershwin Room at the Esplanade Hotel in St Kilda where many of today's big names had their beginnings. So instead of reliving the early experiences of greats such as Mick Molloy or Wil Anderson, I was offered a spot at the Courthouse Theatre in Ballarat – an hour and a half northwest of Melbourne. At first this felt like a nuisance, but the more I thought about it, the more a comedy road trip sounded like fun. Sarah was keen to join me, and we booked a hotel in Ballarat to make a night of it.

RAW applies a strict five-minute time limit and it's important to stick to your 'tight five'. In order to uncover the next wave of great comedians, they rightfully don't tolerate wafflers. This played to my forehand, as I've always been very careful and deliberate with timing, and I measured an adaptation of 'socially awkward' to be exactly five minutes. I practised it multiple times on the journey, and promised Sarah that after this gig I'd focus on writing new material for no better reason than to at least spare her the repetition. (I tried to justify that at some stage John Lennon probably made the same promise to Yoko Ono while practising *Imagine*, but Sarah didn't buy it and just reminded me not to sit on the box of laxatives in my back pocket, as I'd done recently.)

Ballarat was a thriving gold mining town in the nineteenth century and the site of the Eureka Stockade, considered by many to be the birthplace of democracy in Australia. Today its main tourist attraction is Sovereign Hill – a lifelike recreation of the 1850s township complete with actors in period costume and a creek where children can pan for gold. Impressively, much of Ballarat's heritage-listed architecture still reflects the antiquity of the Victorian era. We were to learn that the Courthouse Theatre, which looks decidedly more like the courthouse it used to be rather than the theatre it now is, was recently used as a facade in *The Doctor Blake Mysteries*. By contrast, I'm sure the comedy performed inside it tonight was going to be much more contemporary and innovative.

RAW Comedy was, at this stage, the most professionally organised gig I'd been involved with. Sarah dropped me off for my 6pm call time (even that sounded exciting!) and amused herself around Ballarat for an hour or so while I hung out in the green room (ohh!) with the other comedians and the host, Venezuelan-born comedian Ivan Aristeguieta. I was slightly bemused that I hadn't heard of him, because a sneaky Google search told me he is quite accomplished. The first article that popped up explained he'd been a comedian in his home country but had moved to Australia a few years ago and used comedy as a way to help him learn English. He has since done full festival shows here. It occurred to me what an extraordinary accomplishment it must be to perform comedy in your second language. It's certainly hard enough in your first! Considering that so much of comedy can depend on very specific word choices, subtle inflection and nuances of language, I was immediately in awe of this guy, and I'm not sure whether it was more as a comedian or an English teacher. He was an engaging young man who chatted freely to all competitors and helped us to relax.

Among the other eleven comedians were a couple of people I knew, but it was mostly people I'd never met and it was quickly apparent that some were using this competition as their first actual gig, as in they hadn't even performed open mic. To me that seemed an incredible waste of a RAW entry, as you'd might as well get as good as you can beforehand. I chatted to a young contestant named Alison, an actor trying out comedy for the first time, and she explained that at the time there were no real opportunities for comedians in Ballarat to practise at local open mic, so she was giving this a go. I thought back to my own nervous debut at Station 59 and considered how much more intimidating it would be to perform for the first time here, and congratulated her for her courage.

The only other female comedian was an older lady, probably in her late fifties, with reading glasses on a chain and the demeanour of a librarian. This was her first comedy spot as well. She was nervously going through notes, and explained to me that most of her humour was based on her own life.

'That's wonderful – the best comedy always comes from your own subjective experiences,' I assured her.

As she looked a bit nervous, I shared with her my technique of changing your inner voice to 'I'm excited', which I knew would shortly be of use to me again as the pre-show nerves would kick in. She thanked me and I left her to focus on her act. She seemed an endearing lady and I looked forward to what she had to say.

I was listed as the third act in the second bracket, which was fine as it meant I could relax slightly to enjoy the first half and refocus during the interval. Those of us in the second bracket settled into a position backstage that was suitable for listening to the first. Ivan opened the show with about ten minutes of material, including discussion of his Venezuelan background, and the audience laughed enthusiastically from the start. It felt like a great crowd – about 120 or so we were told – and I was excited for the rare chance to perform in a theatre with curtains, spotlights, a professional MC and a ticketed audience. There was nobody playing pool, no noisy talkers, just a room full of genuine punters wanting to laugh. My only mild concern was sweating too much, as this lovely theatre that retained so much of its original courthouse architecture also seemed to retain its nineteenth century air conditioning, and it was stifling on this February evening. So I drank plenty of water and wore my customary black T-shirt, a common strategy for comedians to hide sweaty armpits – another handy tip I'd picked up from the Lounge workshops.

Ivan reminded the crowd that this was RAW and '...these are new comedians, many of them performing comedy for the first time, so please give them all your laughter.' With that it occurred to me that in the entire theatre, Sarah would be the only person aware that this was not my first gig (presuming she hadn't found something more interesting to do) and the audience should be fairly easy to win over as long as I didn't stuff up. Hopefully the judges would feel the same way.

The first couple of acts were both debutants and delivered admirable first sets. They were clearly nervous and unpolished – nothing the judges were likely to promote to the next round – but since my own disastrous debut at Station 59, I was forever impressed by successful first-timers. They thoroughly deserved their generous laughter and applause.

As the third act was introduced, I turned to the bloke I'd been chatting to for most of the night – a local comedian named Tim Young who was scheduled to be on immediately before me – and commented that the audience seemed well warmed up and the vibe in the theatre was exciting. I think he was about to agree, but before he could do so the air was pierced by a loud, guttural scream. There was a moment of stunned confusion as we all stared at each other blankly. It was a female scream, an anguished one that had come through the speakers and reverberated throughout the antiquated courthouse, and our heads.

'What the fuck?' said the lovely Alison.

Another scream followed, and then something small and white pinged off the side wall, narrowly missing our heads.

'Was that a tooth?' someone blurted in panic.

With trepidation, a few of us peered around the backdrop curtain. The mad screaming woman with the microphone was the librarian. The white thing that had narrowly missed our heads, Sarah informed me later, was a button from her cardigan as she had violently ripped it open. Now that she had engaged the full attention of everyone within the courthouse, and possibly the local constabulary as well, she embarked upon what turned out to be a seven to eight minute rant of fury about her ex-husband. For this period, nobody dared move. The audience sat glued to their seats like 120 school children being berated at assembly. I have little recollection of anything she actually said, and neither does Sarah, such was the shock of her wrath. But what I do remember is that none of it was funny. Not one bit. I don't mean there were failed punchlines, or even just an ironic anti-humour to the whole thing, I mean there was literally nothing placed in the routine for people to laugh at. *Nothing.* It reminded me of Drago at Station 59. A humourless rant that nobody found interesting, let alone funny. But before the show, unbeknown to the audience, she had been scrupulously studying her notes. She'd pored over them just as much as I do when preparing new material. She'd looked nervous and had put a lot of effort into this tirade. So what had she been thinking? Did she honestly believe, 'Gee, they're going to love the bit where I scream and rip open my cardigan spraying the audience with buttons'? Perhaps it was intended to be arty in a way that totally failed on the night. But, more likely, it was just an angry rant, a form of therapy, and this was her best opportunity for a public forum. Whatever the case, it mystifies me as to why some people bother with such abstract material. There might be a place for it in a basement somewhere, but not at RAW. Needless to say, she didn't advance to the next round.

As the show progressed I was beginning to think that, despite my age, I might be a realistic chance to win this heat. While I knew I had only an outside chance of making it all the way to the grand final, winning a heat and progressing one step closer would still be a great honour. After all, *somebody* had to win it, and so far most acts had been good but… well, *raw*, and owing to my experience I knew at this stage my best performance could have them all covered. Selfishly, a part of me now hoped this raw standard would remain for the whole show. In hindsight, I realise it is an incredibly negative mindset to hope for success based on others falling over – pulling a 'Steven Bradbury', as it's now colloquially known – but as I met up with Sarah for some fresh air during the interval, I caught myself thinking it wouldn't be such a bad thing.

(Steven Bradbury was an Australian Winter Olympian who won a speed-skating gold medal in 2002 when every other finalist crashed into a heap before the finish line. Since then his name has become synonymous with winning by default. I've always thought this reputation to be a bit unfair, as Bradbury had worked damn hard to get where he was. Who can get to an Olympic final any other way? And when he assessed his competition in the final, he figured he had little chance of matching them. He has since admitted that his strategy really was to hang behind the pack, as his best opportunity of winning was on the off chance of a pile-up. He played the odds and won. 'Show faith in your own mediocrity' could be his legacy for the world. 'One day the pack might tumble.')

When Tim Young stepped up in the second bracket, he immediately smashed it. A similar age to me, he had a country blokiness about him and the Ballarat audience was laughing heartily. I was very happy for him, and pleased to be following a successful set. So far he was the clubhouse leader and a challenge had been laid down. As he was performing, I was directed to stand in a spot backstage by a woman wearing a headset taking directions from the floor manager (gee I loved this!), and as Tim finished to great applause, Ivan announced my name and she pulled aside the curtain to motion me on stage.

The first thing that hit me was the lights. It's the sign of a reputable gig when you can barely see the audience, and lights were on me from all angles. I could, however, certainly *hear* the audience. While my applause was very welcoming, the walk to the microphone was longer than usual and it kind of dwindled before I got there, leaving me to pick up the mic in silence. In some ways, this was the bit that often caused me the most angst. Comedians normally have only one prop to handle, but it's ridiculous how stressful this can be at the start of a set, especially if the cord needs to be untwined from the stand. I'd never had a major disaster, but on this occasion the cord caught one of the stand's legs and took me a few excruciating seconds of complete silence to untangle. I could sense every set of eyes scrutinising my questionable dexterity, and I'm sure I began to sweat even more. Fortunately, I got the stand away and launched into my routine, and surprisingly Sarah told me afterwards that she hadn't even noticed my struggle. It's strange how time can feel so distorted under the intensity of stage lights.

My routine went very well with good laughs in the right places, and my overall feeling was relief. During Turbo Lax, when I asked the audience which book they thought I'd left hidden behind the toilet, someone promptly called out *'Fifty Shades of Grey!'* – which got a good laugh in itself. 'No sir, but that would have been an appropriate use for it,' I replied, which luckily got an even bigger laugh thanks to some practised spontaneity.

Now I thought Tim and I were probably on a par. Alison was next and she sounded very confident for her first gig, and got wonderful laughs, so we had a third contender. Unintentionally, the second bracket was working out to be of a higher standard than the first. The second last act was a young man who bounded on stage and wooed the audience immediately. He wore a charming vest suit that we'd joked about with him backstage, implying that he was trying to outdo us all in the wardrobe department. Well, it turned out he also outdid us in the humour department. His name was Ethan Cavanagh and he won the heat. He was a thoroughly deserving winner, and an appealing choice for the judges as a young, fresh talent with material that was risqué but clean enough for telly, and a well-defined image. I was happy for him to win as he had the potential to go all the way to Edinburgh. We were all invited back on stage for a collective round of applause and the night concluded as a wonderful success. Audience and comedians alike had enjoyed a great experience and the decision to drive to rural Victoria for a five-minute spot had been well and truly justified.

The audience had been enthusiastic all night. Screaming librarian aside, they had been supportive of all new comedians who they surely viewed as extremely brave. To be fair, it was not a true reflection of how material might go in a more merciless environment, but at least this audience was acknowledging effort and recognising those who had the courage to step up. It would be nice if that was more often the case at other venues. This audience was here to have fun, as comedy audiences should be. (It's never ceased to amaze me how so many people in Melbourne – a city with countless entertainment options – will attend free open mic comedy featuring raw, unpaid comedians, yet sit in the front row with arms folded and a scowl that says, 'Go on, make me laugh!')

Afterwards, Sarah and I joined most of the other comics for drinks and a few games of pool at one of the great local pubs. The camaraderie between our group was palpable. We'd just been through quite an experience together, some for the first time, and it was a relief to unwind and get to know each other. I must admit I now felt quite ashamed of wanting to pull a Steven Bradbury, which reiterated my disdain for competition comedy. It was much better, of course, to be a small part of a wonderful show, than the best comedian on an average night. I was content with my own performance, and delighted to see so many others achieve a life goal tonight. Humour is way too subjective to ever discern true winners, I believe, and if comedy nights turned into sport people would eventually forget why they're really there. They might forget why comedy is so important. It was a pleasure to add to my ever expanding circle of friends in comedy that night.

Driving home the next afternoon, Sarah and I vowed to go on more trips together. This one had been heaps of fun.

'What have you got in mind?' I asked her.

'I don't know,' she replied. 'Somewhere a bit further might be nice. Maybe involving a plane?'

'For sure,' I agreed, although as our last trip had been to Iceland we'd probably been as far away as we could get. 'Is there anywhere you've always wanted to see?'

As it turned out, there was. Sarah had never been to the USA and by now had probably heard enough of my stories to wish I would 'shut up already'. She really wanted to go but had doubts I would too, as my own trip had been only three years earlier. I assured her that was no problem whatsoever! I had loved my time in the States, and there was so much more

I wanted to see. And, of course, it would be even better to go with a partner. We began planning our American adventure before we even got home. Being a pair of teachers was handy, as we both had two weeks of school holidays in July, the ideal time to escape a Melbourne winter.

In fact, as we planned our itinerary, I figured two weeks was just not enough, so I applied for a week of long service leave to extend my trip. Unfortunately, Sarah had not been teaching long enough at this stage to accrue leave, so she settled for the two weeks. She really wanted to see LA and then the beaches of Miami, so that was our plan for the first fortnight, along with a couple of nights in Atlanta. Then she would depart for home while I spent an extra six nights by myself.

'Where would you like to do that?' Sarah asked, but my response needed no thought whatsoever. There was one place I especially needed to see, and I'd vowed to do so upon my next trip to the USA. As the birthplace of stand-up comedy, New York City was calling me. I couldn't wait to check out so many of its famous clubs and hopefully find a stage to perform on.

And what I didn't realise at this moment was that Sarah was about to plan an amazing surprise for me in New York. I would have been content with just checking out a few clubs and hopefully finding an open mic stage. But as a very early birthday present, Sarah was about to plan something even better. For a stand-up comedian, my surprise was to be much, much better indeed.

13

DA BOMB

One of my favourite things about travelling to the northern hemisphere in July is enjoying an extra summer. It feels like cheating the system a bit. I've heard of surfers who chase an endless summer across the world and I wondered if I could ever be that cool. This was perhaps as close as I would get, but lying on beaches in California and Florida while deliberately checking the single-digit temperatures in Melbourne, I couldn't help but feel a little bit gnarly.

In LA we stayed in beachside Santa Monica, more upmarket than my last trip. Our arrival coincided with the fourth of July long weekend, so Sarah's first experience of the United States was a nicely festive one. We did the touristy things in LA, and this time I got a photo of Robin Williams' footprints and handprints outside the Chinese Theatre, which to my delight included a hand-etched 'Carpe Diem', a reference to the iconic *Dead Poets Society* – a film I still like to show my senior English students. We did a Star Tour and I quickly realised that Jorge, our bus driver and tour guide, was the same guy I'd had three years earlier when I'd enjoyed the same tour. He did a great job, but it immediately stood out to me that at every landmark he was making the same jokes as in 2014. There is nothing wrong with that, of course. He has figured out which jokes work best and he's sticking with them. In fact, from a joke-telling point of view, he'd captured the best type of audience – one that is never the same (well, nearly). I've heard this described as the busker's principle – if the audience keeps moving, buskers can play the same song all day. I was actually jealous of this guy! It would be so good to have such solidly tested material and a fresh audience every day. Jorge told us that he'd been a tour guide for more than twenty years and loved his job. I wondered which part he genuinely loved, driving a bus through the hectic LA traffic or getting a guaranteed laugh?

I persuaded Sarah that we needed to go back to *The Bomb Shelter*. Leading up to this trip, she'd heard a lot about what a great time I'd had there and the wonderful people I'd met. I held out hope that some might even be there again and possibly remember me. What a fun night we could have reminiscing and hearing the great new material we'd all come up with! During the afternoon I went through my notes. I figured instead of using my most recent routines from home I would rework the bits that had worked so well last time. Even though they'd been fairly spontaneous, I was now crafting them into a more rehearsed version that once again drew upon cultural differences between Australia and America, observations that could only work with my out-of-town perspective.

When we got to the Hollywood Hotel, I was disappointed to learn the comedy nights were no longer held in the downstairs bar. We were directed to a smaller room farther away, in what felt more like a business function area. It had a temporary stage set up and immediately lacked the atmosphere of its previous existence. And it was no longer referred to as *The Bomb Shelter*. I recognised nobody from last time. In fact, the group of about thirty or so were all very young and seemed to know each other well. We almost felt like somebody's parents crashing a party. Sarah must have been wondering why I'd been so excited to return! We said hello to a couple of guys at a table as we took seats, and they were quite friendly and identified us straight away as Australians. I'd been noticing that, unlike last time, my accent was not so foreign to Americans now. One of the guys mentioned that Jim Jefferies was his favourite comedian, and I wondered if Jim had become the next Paul Hogan in so far as making the Aussie accent more familiar here.

The young woman running the show didn't exactly go out of her way to welcome me as I put my name on the list. In fact, she was very clear that I had only four minutes, even after I implored that I'd flown over 1500 miles for this. As the show progressed I sensed she was in a hurry to get through it, as though she and her buddies had somewhere else to be. But as I sat waiting on deck I was confident that my refreshing Aussie persona was going to floor them again, so much so that they wouldn't even worry about time limits and flashing lights.

I bounded up on stage, introduced myself with an exaggerated 'G'day', and got some laughs for my opening couple of lines. But as I was about to launch into the rest of my material, some of which I'd been waiting three years to repeat, something completely unexpected happened.

I blanked out.

Bizarrely, I completely forgot where to go with this routine. As my brain fumbled for the next line, every second felt like a minute. The harder I tried to find anything even close to what I'd been planning to say, the harder it became. It is truly one of the most awful experiences you can have on stage. To relate, imagine being in a completely dark room. It's really,

really dark – pitch black. And it's a large room. Now, somewhere in this room are your car keys, and you need to find them urgently. That's what it feels like to blank out on stage.

I could feel the intense glare of every person in the room. It was humiliating. Eventually I composed myself and continued with another part of my routine, but by now I'd lost my mojo. I couldn't deliver any lines with confidence and clearly had been unable to engage the audience. Remarkably, I managed to squeeze out a couple more small laughs, but as I resorted to more trusted material that could have won them back a little, I could hear music. It was rap music and it was getting louder. It was quite distracting. Where was it coming from? No wait... really? Was I being *played off*?

To any performing artist, being played off stage is the ultimate indignity. It's as though the young MC had decided to bypass the flashing light altogether to make extra sure I didn't linger.

Sarah and I soon left. I was shattered that *The Bomb Shelter* of my memory no longer existed, and devastated with my performance. Forgetting material has always been a much greater fear for me than not getting laughs, but until this point it had never happened. I'd delivered many performances that could have been funnier, but my overriding feeling afterwards had always been how well I'd done to at least remember everything. I'd begun to think of my memory as a strength and that blanking out would never happen. Now I'd proved otherwise, and the spectre of forgetting material would be hovering above me on stage from now on, heckling me as I was telling myself I'm doing ok. This was a big deal.

Back at Santa Monica Pier, we watched the sunset at our new favourite outdoor bar (it was only dusk, such was our hurried exit). There is something unique about a Californian sunset. It seems to last a bit longer than usual, bathing the world in gold as the light is simply in no hurry to slip away. Normally I'd be loving such a scene, but as I stared at the long shadows on the beach with the distant sounds of fun echoing from the amusement park at the end of the pier, all I could think about was how badly I'd just bombed. Sarah tried to encourage me. She was correct in pointing out that I was not as well prepared for a comedy spot as I normally would be; I hadn't practised much, it had been a long time since I'd done that material and I was in holiday mode. All of those reasons made sense, but still, I'd lost a lot of confidence tonight. It had taken me a long time to finally feel confident on the comedy stage, and now I'd taken a massive step backwards in just one night. As much as I valued Sarah's analysis, as she'd unwittingly become quite an authority on bad comedy, I needed some reassurance from a more experienced source, so I did something a bit unusual. I texted Evan. I'm sure wherever he was at about 3pm on a wintry Thursday in Melbourne, he wouldn't have been expecting a message from Santa Monica. However, he was very understanding and we had a bit of a chat via text.

I took comfort when Evan said it had happened to him too. If he'd replied, 'HAHAHA LOL that's a shocker mate what's it like?' I might have quit comedy in that instant. But he explained it happens to us all and I shouldn't worry too much about it. When he pointed out that 'it feels like you're up there for an hour', I instantly related. He added that at times he would use a bit of crowd work until he remembered where he was going, or else just go on with another joke. He recommended doing more MC work to develop crowd work skills for those moments. In a way it was comforting to know it sometimes happens to the best comics too, and I was realising yet again how skilful and professional the best need to be. Evan advised to 'always have a joke loaded to go', which made sense. It would be good to have an emergency joke in my back pocket that could work in any context. I thanked Evan and looked forward to resuming the conversation in person back home.

Importantly, this moment did not detract from an otherwise wonderful holiday for me and Sarah in LA. We both left with great memories. But it did play on my mind a lot, and I vowed to never again be caught in the spotlight.

Our holiday next took us to the east side of America, which was as new to me as it was to Sarah. Atlanta was our first stop, and admittedly we were only detouring here for two nights in order to see my favourite band, Metallica. I'd seen them in Melbourne of course, but to see a concert in America was just next level cool! It was a detour we both enjoyed very much.

On the journey I learned that Atlanta is only the thirty-ninth most populous city in the USA, which surprised me, as it hosted the 1996 Olympic Games. That gives insight into the enormous scale of this country. For comparison, according to Wikipedia, the thirty-ninth most populous city in Australia is Dubbo.

I'd love to see the Dubbo Olympics. But good luck getting a dinner booking at the pub for that fortnight.

Miami was next, and this was all about relaxing. It gets to a point on some travels where you feel as though you need a holiday from your holiday. It can be deceptively unrelaxing to spend a lot of time flying and navigating new cities, and sometimes you feel like just plonking on a beach or beside a pool, which is what we did here for several blissful days. Sarah and I really loved visiting Little Havana, and for some reason I bought a Cuban cigar the size of my forearm.

On our last day in Miami, I bade farewell to Sarah as she flew home and I went in the opposite direction to New York. It was sad to part, but I was certainly going to be busy. Sarah's early birthday present to me was a four-day workshop at the American Comedy Institute (ACI), where I would have the chance to workshop material in group settings, similarly to the Lounge, but also in one-on-one sessions with a professional. The workshop would culminate with a performance at the famous Gotham Comedy Club in front of a paying New York audience. I was floored by this amazingly unique and thoughtful gift. A more exciting comedy experience I could not have asked for, and my gratitude has always been difficult to put into words. Sarah and I said goodbye at the airport with a warm embrace as she went home to our regular world, and I embarked towards an exciting new one.

My main challenge now was to put my LA performance out of mind. I was preparing for the biggest gig of my life so far on the back of my worst. It wasn't going to be easy.

14

BIG APPLE

It's a strange sensation to travel to the other side of the world and feel completely familiar with your new surroundings. Such is our exposure to New York City through TV and film that I immediately felt as though I'd been here before. Yellow cabs, crowded streets, incessant honking, hot dogs with mustard – I loved every part of it straight away. And there is a rudeness to people here that is distinctly New York. Not a *bad* rudeness, just the type that evolves in a small space shared by over eight million people. For example, New Yorkers rarely say thank you when you hold open a door, and if you want baloney in your sandwich, you don't smile politely and say, 'I'll grab some baloney on that please, cheers mate, tah.' You say, *'Gimme baloney!'* It just takes some getting used to.

    I arrived at my Manhattan hotel in the late afternoon and spent the rest of the daylight ambling through nearby Central Park, one of the world's great city parks. Even as an Australian I was impressed by the size of it. And on this superb summer's afternoon it was typically packed. There were people *everywhere*; jogging, cycling, walking dogs, throwing Frisbees, playing softball, soccer or volleyball, reading, snoozing, cuddling, painting, playing on equipment, rollerblading, laughing at street performers, sailing toy boats or, like me, just strolling around and taking it all in. In a district where almost everybody lives in an apartment without a backyard, this was where they would go outside. This was where children would play and poets would write. This was Manhattan's backyard, and it was magnificent.

One building next to the park caught my attention for its unusual architecture and instant familiarity. Google promptly told me that 55 Central Park West was one of the first buildings on the Upper West Side to be heavily influenced by the Art Deco movement, and had been home to many famous artists and musicians. Still that wasn't ringing any bells, so I scrolled further to find it was also the main apartment building used in *Ghostbusters*. That was it! It's where the boys had fought Gozer and blown up Stay Puft the Marshmallow Man!

The next day was my only available full day of sight-seeing before the workshop began, so I attempted as much as possible. My first tour guide reminded us that New York was divided into five boroughs: Manhattan, Brooklyn, The Bronx, Queens and Staten Island. For the first time it occurred to me how the *Five Boroughs* comedy night in Hardware Lane, Melbourne, derived its name. It was in honour of the spiritual home of stand-up comedy. It would be too difficult to see all five boroughs while I was here. In fact, I never left Manhattan, but that was ok because you could spend months in New York's innermost borough and never get bored.

My first point of call was the 9/11 memorial site. I'd always wondered what it would feel like to stand in the footprints of the former World Trade Centre and I could immediately feel the weight of emotion forever attached to it. On the site now are two large water features that trace the perimeter of the former towers, two perpetual waterfalls symbolising renewal. The area is nicely shaded by white oaks, selected for their resilience to all conditions. I was pleased that it wasn't crowded with people taking selfies and the ever present T-shirt sellers. I walked slowly around both memorial pools and viewed the names of the nearly 3000 victims. There can be something dehumanising about numbers, but by seeing the endless array of individual names inscribed upon the bronze parapets, I was beginning to feel the story of each human life. I was glad to finally have the chance to visit this site, and the extremely well presented (and crowded) 9/11 Memorial Museum, as it had been something I'd felt compelled to do since watching the horrors unfold on live TV back in 2001.

What I also remembered from that time was one person who seemed to nurse New York back into a state of relative normality – David Letterman. He was at the height of his popularity as host of *The Late Show* when tragedy struck, and suddenly nobody felt like laughing any more. Perhaps when you and your writers routinely make people laugh for so long, you adopt a strong – maybe even paternal – sense of responsibility when laughs are truly needed. When one of the world's greatest cities mourns, it will turn to its trusted comedians as a gauge for when it's ok to laugh again. And Letterman handled it perfectly. On September 17, in his first show after the attack, he addressed the city in a broken voice and praised the virtues of police officers and firefighters, and all those who were lost. He contemplated whether he should 'even do a show at all', but determined it was important to do so. It was hard not to cry as he maintained how 'terribly sad' the feeling was around the city. But a couple of minutes into his monologue he made a joke. It was a subtle joke aimed at his long-time musical director and straight man Paul Schaffer, taking aim as usual at his receding hairline. The audience understood the relationship between the two and knew it was ok to laugh here. It was a masterstroke. His audience needed to feel safe in laughing again, and a standard crack at his friend's shiny dome was as cliche as it comes, but it welcomed the audience back into a state of normality, which was seen by millions. A few minutes later he made another joke, and the audience laughed even more. At the end he made a final gag about his friend and fellow TV host Regis Philbin and the audience laughed in earnest – a genuine laugh in which the weight of sadness could be felt to lift, even if just for a second.

With one show, Letterman told America it's still ok to laugh. He demonstrated the ways in which laughter can be an act of defiance. It was testament to the fact that people always *want* to laugh.

The American Comedy Institute is located on the fifth floor of the New Yorker Hotel, on a famous corner opposite Pennsylvania (Penn) Station and Madison Square Gardens.

Upon arrival I shared an elevator with an attractive young woman, probably in her late twenties, with whom I endured one of those elevator silences that becomes awkward upon realising you're going to the same place. Her name was Olga Namer, and I didn't know it yet, but she had been raised by an Orthodox Jewish family in Brooklyn, one that had done its best to 'protect' her from the harsh secular world. There was an expectation from Olga's parents that she would live her life within the confines of their strict religious community. But, as I was soon to discover, Olga couldn't do that. Why? Because she was funny. She had an innate desire to make people laugh.

She had a funny voice inside her, and – much to her parents' chagrin – it was pushing its way out.

That's where Stephen Rosenfield comes into it.

Stephen is the director of the ACI and has been coach and mentor of many comedians who have made it to professional status. A recent alumnus was Jim Gaffigan, who had recently become known to Australians through the eponymously titled *The Jim Gaffigan Show*. Stephen's CV states that many of his students have starred in movies, TV series, commercials, Broadway productions and their own radio programs. They have become writers, actors and producers. It was occurring to me how stand-up can lead to so many other great pathways that seemed otherwise impossible to break into. Many of these graduates went through the ACI's full time year-long program, which sounds like a massive commitment, but I guess if you're aiming to be professional it's no different to enrolling in any other tertiary course. It really highlighted to me how American comedy is truly an industry. Stephen has vast experience in both comedy and theatre, and has been a lecturer in comedy at major universities across America. *The New York Times* describes him as 'The best known comedy teacher in the country'.

When meeting Stephen, he doesn't immediately strike you as someone who would be an expert on stand-up. In his sixties with a distinguished grey beard, he is softly spoken with a calm demeanour, and he articulates himself with the fewest words needed in order to make a strong statement. Perhaps years of coaching comedians to do the same has worn off on him.

For my first session I was introduced to half a dozen others who were beginning the four-day course. We had a quick briefing from Stephen and then watched a ninety-minute film, a montage of some of his lectures on comedy. I took copious notes, feeling very much as though I was back at uni and loving the experience. His recorded lectures began by going through some of the basics, such as the different styles of comedy (observational, anecdotal, put down…) and comedian types (character based, comically flawed, edgy…), as well as a lot of terminology pertaining to the craft of comedy writing, such as 'act out' (when a comedian acts out a scenario within a monologue, often playing multiple roles) and 'call back' (a reference to an earlier joke, often used to close a set). I knew most of this already, but it was still insightful to hear Stephen discussing these styles and techniques in depth.

In fact, he was so engrossing I almost forgot we were watching a video. But before long one of the other students, a woman slightly younger than me, began shifting restlessly in her seat, demonstrating all the body language of a bored teenager. She hadn't taken any notes at all. The video soon ended and I introduced myself. Her name was Joan, an evangelical pastor from Wisconsin here to develop humourist skills for use in her sermons. What a wonderful endeavour, I thought. However, she seemed to have a rather impatient attitude. And as she had never performed stand-up before, I had no idea how she was going to put together a five-minute set for the Gotham Club by the end of the week. It would be interesting to observe how this played out.

After the video, Stephen returned and spoke to us about the four days ahead and explained a few rules. From the outset, he made it abundantly clear that 'generic' humour was to be avoided at all costs. To reiterate his point, he explained the need to say 'No' at a dinner party.

'"Tell us a joke" is the request, or challenge, you will invariably hear when introduced as a comedian in a social situation,' he explained, and I immediately related to it. 'The first thing to learn is that you should *never* abide by this request. First, let's examine why they're asking. They want to hear a joke they can retell to others to get a laugh.' He then emphasised that this is not the style of humour that would make us successful comedians. 'A joke that anyone can tell at a dinner party is the definition of a generic joke.' From early on, this set the tone for the rest of the workshop. Generic material was *outlawed*. Stephen explained that comedy was about stamping material with your own personality, opinions and attitudes to a point where nobody could perform it as successfully as you. At a dinner party, jokes would lack context, technique and persona. If you're doing a joke that would work just as well at a dinner party as it would on stage, it's not worth keeping. He then challenged us to immediately go through our material and cross out anything that was generic – *anything* that could be told just as effectively by most other people. It was a confronting task, as I realised that even though I'd developed a growing awareness of being subjective, a lot of my material still bordered on that category.

Later that evening was our first group workshop. It was set up in a small function room with a makeshift stage in front of an ACI backdrop curtain. Fifteen of us were seated in three rows of chairs, and Stephen sat at a desk behind us. The workshops would run similarly to the Comic's Lounge, but with a more formal structure. Everybody had ten minutes to run through material in front of the group – it could be a full routine or just whatever you wanted to try. Then Stephen would give his feedback, followed by an opportunity for others to do the same. Stephen set strict rules about attentiveness; it was mandatory for us all to focus on each performer instead of our own notes, and nobody was allowed to leave early unless there was an exceptional circumstance (I got the impression this was at very least a life-threatening illness). Phones could be used only for recording your own material and its feedback, and turned completely off at all other times. This may sound overly strict, but I loved it. Stephen created an environment in which every performer had the fullest attention from every audience member, understanding how rare that can be. From early on, he maintained the only *true* feedback is audience laughter.

First up was Olga, who was part of the year-long program. (Our workshop group was a mixture of all students, whether they be enrolled for a year or a week, and the combination seemed to work well for everyone.) Olga told of her dilemma in introducing her non-Jewish boyfriend to her ultra-Orthodox parents. 'If you continue dating him we're going to disown you,' she said, acting out. 'Then immediately I was like… "Oh my God, what?… We have money?"' This got a great laugh from the group and tremendous praise from Stephen. He made a point to us newbies that it was the perfect example of non-generic material. Olga was the only person in the room who could do that bit.

When it was my turn I made a diabolical error of judgement. On the plane from Melbourne I'd thought of a joke that involved, well, let's just say masturbation as a form of in-flight entertainment. I'm not going to repeat the joke here because I'm hoping it will disappear from this earth (although it is related to the old cliche of flying a long way and having 'tired arms'). But at the time I thought it was worth trying, despite its crassness, and to be fair it did get a decent laugh after I introduced myself as an Australian and complained about how long and boring the flight had been. Then I did my whole socially awkward routine. I returned to my seat as Stephen stepped up before the class with clipboard in hand. The best known comedy teacher in America opened his mouth to begin his feedback and then paused, as though struggling with some of the images I had just presented him. Then he spoke in a slow and measured voice.

'I'm going to address your opening. You know… the first thing that comes out of your mouth is kind of like your comedy identity. It gives the audience a picture of who you are.' He paused again, allowing my first image to resurface in the minds of the audience. 'And I'm not sure that you want that picture. I'm not sure that's who you are, from what I'm hearing.'

He was absolutely right. How did I not see that? After so much discussion about generic humour, I had opened with a wanking gag.

'When you bring out the fact there was nothing else to do on the plane except masturbate… they *believe* you. Unless you make it absolutely clear that what you're doing is fanciful, they believe you.' By this stage we were all seeing the funny side of my predicament, and Stephen kept going with an act out of his own.

'So I'm out for the night at a comedy club, I'm thinking "ok great here's a new guy from Australia, I wonder what he's like… oh, he masturbated on the plane." At this stage they *believe* that.'

'I believed it,' quipped another comedian.

'So I guess part of what I'm saying is sometimes a laugh is not worth it. If it's throwing off the way you want to be perceived by your audience, even if it gets a laugh, it may not be worth it. I'm questioning whether you want that to be the first impression the audience has of you.'

'Um... no,' I said. 'You're absolutely right, Stephen. Thank you.'

Then he addressed my *Hardcore Pawn* bit. While this had been working well within my socially awkward routine, I'd rewritten it for an American audience and it now involved calling my dear mother from my hotel room and telling her what I'm watching, which leads to a terrible misunderstanding as she is shocked to think that America had morally corrupted me within hours. I even took some liberty with this audience by pretending I hadn't previously seen the show from Australia. I thought this would work well, but what I didn't consider was a difference in pronunciation here, something comedians need to be aware of overseas, particularly if it's the essence of your joke. In Australia, 'pawn' and 'porn' are homophones, but in the US 'pawn' is softer with an elongated vowel and they can tell the difference. Stephen quickly pointed out this problem with my accent.

'At first all I understood was you were sitting in your hotel room watching some hard porn, immediately after masturbating all the way from Australia. We genuinely believe that you're enjoying the porn. And then you decided to call your *mother* to tell her all about it? "Hi Mom, guess what I'm doing now?" Again, I'm not sure that's the identity you want to create for yourself.'

By this stage I was probably turning red. The group was loving his jocularity, no one more than me, but I was receiving an important message as well — one that Stephen would reiterate throughout the week. That is, focus on your persona. That's much more important than being 'jokey', he would stress, as it is not worth compromising your identity just to get a laugh or two. For me, the message of being consistent to my persona was beginning to appear, well, consistently, and it was something I had to focus on. Due to time, Stephen said we would discuss the rest of my material tomorrow in our first private session. (Of the various professional comedians and writers mentoring in this program, I was very lucky to have drawn Stephen himself.) But my objective was becoming clear. I didn't want to stand up at the Gotham Club at the end of the week and repeat an open mic set, I wanted to develop my material and deliver the most personable, non-generic routine I've ever done.

I was looking forward to my first one-on-one session with Stephen, but at the same time it felt incredibly daunting. It was odd that performing in front of just one person could feel more intimidating than a hundred. While Stephen is a benevolent man, right now he was being paid to be my harshest critic. He has worked closely with some of America's best comedians, and getting a genuine laugh from him would be the equivalent of a packed Comic's Lounge.

He greeted me warmly and asked me to revise a couple of my bits from the previous night. In the same performance space as yesterday, I began with Turbo Lax, complete with the small box of fake laxatives I'd carried across the Pacific. Despite the lack of audience, I was happy with the animation of my delivery and finished with an emotional flourish on the punchline, 'Will you save your soul or your pants?'

The brief silence that followed was not a bad one, but it lingered just a tad longer than I felt comfortable with. As Stephen reclined in contemplation I could sense the words forming in his mind. He was here as a coach, not a punter, and as a man who is always careful and measured with his commentary, he was searching for the most insightful analysis possible.

'You're an *asshole*,' he said.

'Oh.'

'What did this guy do to you to deserve that?'

'Um... well, that's why I emphasised his double standards,' I explained. 'I needed a reason for the audience to see him as somebody annoying, they could probably relate that behaviour to people they know.'

'Yes, but that's not enough to make this poor guy *shit his pants*.' I was beginning to love Stephen's understated way of discussing crass and ridiculous topics in a serious manner. 'He hasn't done enough to deserve that, it's horrible. The audience is going to think you're a *jerk* for doing that. Again, that's not the image you want for yourself, is it?'

'Um... no,' I conceded, 'of course not. Thanks for making that clear to me. Do you think the bit is fixable?'

Stephen thought pensively again. He had already stated that we should never throw material away until it's been properly workshopped, so it had potential. But an additional problem was this story's length. We spoke for a bit about anecdotal comedy, and about how a long story needs to be divided into 'subjects'. With each subject along the way there are opportunities to set up and punch. For example, as Stephen explained, when I say I have a Christian housemate, that's my first subject – *punch!* Then my next subject is his double standards – he goes out drinking all night and then expects to just repent – *punch!* And so on. I did have laughs along the way, but he explained it needed stronger hits. A lengthy anecdote needs to be punctuated with big laughs, which I'd have to work on more, as here it's not enough to just build up to one big laugh at the end. In a laid back pub such as Station 59, anecdotes of sixty to ninety seconds don't feel that long, but on a professional stage in the rapid-fire comedy environment of New York, it's a lifetime.

'Have you heard of the laughs per minute ratio?' he asked.

'The LPM?' I joked. 'No.'

'That's right – we can call it the LPM. And right now, the LPM you should be aiming at is four – as in at least four laughs per minute. It doesn't need to be one every fifteen seconds of course, but you know what I mean. Aim for an average of four.'

'Ok,' I said. 'What do professionals aim for?'

'I tell my students that in order to get work as a professional comic, you must regularly achieve six to eight laughs per minute.'

Wow. I let that sink in for a moment. Six to eight laughs per minute sounded tough, but as I reflected on my favourite routines it seemed an accurate guide. And these need to be good laughs, not just chuckles from a couple of tables. Stephen explained that the only exception to this might be in a longer performance of thirty minutes or more. Sometimes the audience needs to take a slight break from laughing, which is where a longer anecdote might be better placed. But within a five-minute set, it's ridiculous to spend over a minute getting to a punchline.

I thanked Stephen for his great advice. As much as I valued my Turbo Lax bit, and as much as it could have been improved, I never performed it again. The bit that had started so well at the Brunny died this day at the New Yorker Hotel. It was true that I did not come across as being very likeable in this story, no matter how I tried to spin it. Likeability, I was learning, is so important. In my other short anecdotes I'm placing myself in a struggle, I am the victim and the audience is 'rooting' for me, as Stephen observed. But in the Turbo Lax routine I undo all of that good work. And overall I wanted to be a cleaner comic anyway.

Stephen asked to see some of my other material. He quite liked it in bits and pieces, but generally he had much the same advice.

'Too jokey – it's not who you want to be perceived as.'

'Too long. Trim the fat.'

'Make the set up shorter. Get to the punch.'

One of his favourite lines of mine was from the story in which a policeman pulls me over believing I was talking on my phone. He commented that this anecdote had great potential, but I was not identifying the punchline properly.

'Where's the laugh?' he asked. It was a phrase to be asked often of myself and other comics over the next few days. I explained the punchline was when the policeman didn't believe that my joke was worthy of a comedian and gave me a ticket.

'No, it's not' Stephen replied.

'It isn't?'

'That's not the part that gets the biggest reaction from your audience. Did you not notice last night, the biggest laugh was for your next line, when you said "Great, I was getting a ticket and a heckle"?'

'Really? I thought that was maybe just because it was a room full of comedians.'

'No,' said Stephen with a hearty chuckle, 'it's a very funny line. Any audience would laugh at that.' I could tell his laughter was real – it would be implausible for a man of his experience to fake laughter by now. He acted out the joke in a neurotic style, emphasising the frustration of it all, and I swear if I closed my eyes I could have been listening to Woody Allen. It sounded so much better from him, and after hearing his performance of my material I was amazed I'd actually written it.

'Remember – always identify where the *laugh* is. Then work backwards from there.'

I had three hours between the private session and tonight's group session in which I was expected to perform again and demonstrate sharper writing. It was a sweltering day and the streets were oppressively crowded, so rather than returning to my hotel I decided to settle into an air-conditioned rooftop bar across the road, overlooking Madison Square Gardens. I ordered a drink and some food, took out my exercise book and pen, and for a moment enjoyed a wonderful New York view. While I'm sure I couldn't tolerate such busyness on a permanent basis, there was something about the New York bustle that I loved. Every person within the throng was an individual with a story. Everyone had somewhere to go. It fascinated and excited me that so many stories could coexist in such close proximity.

As I was daydreaming, two men in business suits sat at the table next to mine. They ate lunch, conducted a meeting and left all within fifteen minutes. They appeared to work in sales and were discussing shifting units of alcohol. What a great example of stories coexisting, I thought. A few feet away were two guys feeling the pressure of meeting quotas for the sale of alcohol, while I was here writing jokes to become a comedian, giving people a target to hurl abuse at while consuming it.

15

GOTHAM

In front of the group at the New Yorker Hotel that evening, I was much happier with my material. I'd made it much tighter, cutting as many unnecessary words as I could. Stephen was so adamant about keeping set-ups as concise as possible without compromising the punch that it became mildly obsessive for the whole group. When people were nervously going through notes before a session, they weren't trying to remember material – they were scrutinising it for superfluous words. It reminded me of an activity I use every year to prepare students for essay writing. I instruct them to write a passage about what they did on the weekend, the only rule being it has to be exactly fifty words. Then, they are required to reduce the passage to its lowest possible word count without changing any of its meaning. It can be fun and competitive, and students will regularly end up cutting at least half their words without compromising the message. In fact, the message often becomes stronger. The same principle is vital to good comedy.

And, most importantly, I made my routine as non-generic as possible. I told my anecdotes as myself, highlighting my own perspectives and vulnerabilities, and was careful not to be 'jokey'. Even though I'd performed most of this material to the same group last night, it was received with much better laughter.

'Good for you, Ben,' appraised Stephen proudly, 'good for you.' He offered more feedback and noted we would discuss it further in our second private session the following day. I took my seat feeling a sense of accomplishment. And fortunately I had performed early tonight, so I could now relax and comfortably observe the work of others. I was learning just as much from their feedback as my own.

The pastor from Wisconsin was struggling a bit to find her comedic footing. Joan had come to New York with no background in comedy and I wondered if this would be a waste of her time and money. But Stephen understood this and encouraged her to just talk, to tell us about herself with no pressure to be funny. So she told us about her life as a Lutheran missionary, and her experiences of spreading the gospel around her home state and beyond (last night I'd been careful not to make eye contact with her during my bible/toilet paper punchline). She had confidence and I began to warm to her personality. I felt she could make a good comedian if she wanted to be one. As she spoke there were some moments of slight self-deprecation, and Stephen picked up on these and encouraged her to develop funny punchlines around them. He explained how self-deprecating humour can be endearing to an audience, a style of comedy made famous by legends such as Phyllis Diller.

'Ultimately, what gives an audience the licence to laugh at your problems is the fact that you're ok with them,' he said, reminding me of lessons I'd learned from the Lounge.

'Comedy can be like a forum for unvarnished truth' he continued. 'It's a place where we can openly face our imperfections, weaknesses and fears.' I was impressed he had immediately seen

Joan's comic potential out of seemingly nowhere and given her a style to work with.

In addition, there were some more experienced new comedians doing the year-long course and it was fascinating to learn beside them. Rosco Nash was a very funny guy about my age who has since become well known locally for his 'blue collar New York attitude', as I've read in his reviews. Likewise, Joey Rimatello, slightly older, was emerging with a clear 'Brooklyn' style. The Brooklyn accent is the distinctly urban sound of Andrew Dice Clay (best known outside of stand-up for playing Ford Fairlane) and just about any henchman called Tony. Laura Bassi was a young woman working as a babysitter, 'which means I change diapers all day and then wipe the babies with my bachelor's degree.' Stephen regularly quoted Laura as another who achieves likability by placing herself in a struggle. Similarly, Aise O'Neil was only recently out of high school, but already had a well-developed persona as a slightly deadpan, awkward guy who was comfortable joking about his autism. On stage he wore an ill-fitting suit and claimed, 'My high school was famous for having the state's highest suicide rate. Which was great because I love a challenge.'

It was striking to see how all of Stephen's longer-term mentees had developed such independent styles and clearly defined personas. It would have been fascinating to see old footage of their first performances in this same room, to see if they'd started from as far back as me with a plane-wanking joke. I was learning so much from everybody here and could feel my insight into comedy developing steadily. Stephen's coaching style was direct and honest, exactly what I needed. And while I did chuckle to myself at how strictly he ran the room (at one stage between acts I was questioned for standing to stretch my legs), on some level I loved being in the classroom again. While someone on the other side of the globe was filling in for me this week as a teacher, I was expanding my mind as a student. It reinforced my belief that when we find passions in life, we should never stop learning.

The following day in our private session Stephen carefully read through my notes. He now asked that we write material word-for-word on paper, underlining the expected laughs. While reading, he smiled encouragingly and said, 'Good, Ben. The rewrites have worked well. Much less generic and more of *you* coming through. And you can see what a difference it makes to trim the fat.'

'Absolutely,' I agreed. 'It was great advice to take out anything that was not a laugh or directly setting up a laugh. There's really no point in keeping anything else.'

'Indeed.'

He continued to read, when a more concerned look crossed his face.

'Oh no, what's the matter?' I thought. I was hoping he'd get through my whole routine with nothing but praise.

'Vegan blowjob,' he said, pronouncing the words slowly and letting them hang in the air. My heart sank a notch, as this was one of my favourite bits. It was always guaranteed a big laugh. I'd used it as a closer many times. What could possibly be wrong with it?

'It's a very funny joke,' he clarified without a hint of a smile, 'but it's too jokey.' I think he could see my disappointment, so he continued. 'It's a funny premise, but how exactly are you likable in this anecdote?'

'Well, I'm placing myself in a struggle,' I explained. 'It's typical of my dumb luck to get home and miss out due to something so innocuous as dietary requirements.'

Stephen nodded in agreement, but told me it still wasn't fitting my overall persona. He explained that so far I was coming across as a likeable guy in his forties, comically down on his luck, who was now suddenly and inexplicably focused on sex. 'You're placing the importance of this above the relationship,' he highlighted, questioning whether that was the image I wanted for myself.

'Of course not,' I replied. Again, I'd sacrificed image and persona to get a laugh – albeit a really good laugh – and been blind to the way audiences were perceiving me overall.

'Remember, Ben, at this stage the audience still *believes* you. Do you really want them to see you this way?'

'No I don't, but how can we fix it? I really don't want to throw this one away, it's one of my favourite bits.'

'That's fine,' Stephen reassured, 'we can work with it.'

After some deep thought, he discussed placing the dilemma within the context of a relationship. Perhaps my partner decides to become a vegan, and sacrificing oral sex was my way to support her. And it would have to be genuine and thoughtful, not sarcastic or resigned. It would draw upon an element of being comically flawed. Stephen and I had some good laughs between us as we threw around ideas as to how this was, in the guy's mind, the sweetest and most romantic gesture he's ever made. In the end I loved the idea, but it would take some work and experimentation to write it well. I thanked Stephen for his vision.

'That's ok, Ben, this is all part of the journey to discover your true identity as a comedian. Remember, you need to be emotionally full on stage. This is the key to creating a persona. It can take many years to crystalise who you are.'

Over the next couple of days I did little else but focus on preparing for Friday night's performance at the Gotham Club. There was so much more of New York City I wanted to see, but it would need to wait until next time. I hadn't even ridden the subway yet – which seemed culturally remiss – but as everything I needed was within a thirty-minute walk of my hotel, I had no need to venture underground.

My immediate problem was, now that I'd rewritten my favourite bits to be more concise, my routine as a whole had gone from five minutes to three. My LPM was higher but it left my mileage short. Stephen told us that it doesn't matter if we don't use our full five minutes on stage, but cutting short my time allowance was unthinkable to me. This was possibly a once in a lifetime opportunity to perform at a famous New York comedy club, and I was going to enjoy every second of it.

'Alright, what else have you got?' he said.

I had plenty of other bits in various stages of development that I was keen to workshop with him. One was about losing weight, which I thought he would like because it was nicely subjective.

'I'm trying to lose weight so I'm making some positive lifestyle changes,' I said, feeling slightly more relaxed before my one-person audience. 'For example, every day now, every single day... instead of driving, I now walk to the liquor store.' (I was relieved to deliver this as intended, because back home I normally say 'Dan Murphy's'.)

'Hmm,' said Stephen, 'it's not as strong as your other stuff.' I was beginning to recognise this as his polite form of derision.

'I think part of it is you're not overweight enough to do fat jokes.'

I should point out at this stage of life I was becoming increasingly conscious of the midlife bulge, which had by now been exacerbated by three weeks of American food. And while I was disappointed that Stephen didn't immediately like my routine about trying to lose weight, I was in equal part delighted for the bodily compliment.

'Oh really?' I said. 'Thank you very much.'

'Here's what I'm saying, Ben. You don't appear to be overweight. Maybe in your eyes you are, and technically you might be, but you don't immediately strike the audience as somebody who needs to lose weight.'

'At least not enough to do fat jokes?'

'That's right.'

I was so thrilled by this observation that I almost posted it on Facebook. But it made good sense, as when I recall comedians who have cornered the fat joke market their weight is obvious. In fact, I've often wondered if they maintain their weight just to do the jokes!

'Maybe I could take a different approach,' I suggested. 'What if I leave the weight out of it? What if I talk about turning forty, about how this is an age where you really need to start looking after your health a lot more. This is an age where your body can insist you make some lifestyle changes.'

'Yes,' said Stephen positively. 'Good. That could work.'

'Best to go with what you've got,' I agreed.

'I'm over forty, I'm trying to get healthy,' said Stephen, acting out my routine, 'So I've made some real lifestyle changes. For example, now every day instead of driving… I'm walking to the liquor store.'

I was in awe, once again, of how he had immediately made it sound funnier than I did. He advised me to hit 'every day' and to relocate the slight pause. He had a sharp instinct for the seemingly minor details and explained these can make a crucial difference. I thought back to the Comic's Lounge where I'd heard the same said of Jerry Seinfeld, who supposedly scrutinises every word, every inflection – rewriting and practising each bit until word-for-word perfect.

Stephen asked if I'd written anything new since being in New York. I'd drafted a couple of observational bits, one about the obscenely large lottery prizes in America ('$80 million? You could buy Australia for that! And still have change for New Zealand!') which he loved and encouraged me to keep for the Gotham Club, and another about travelling in general and the potential embarrassment of being contacted by your bank for irregular credit card activity. The idea had come to me in Miami when Sarah had asked whether I'd informed my bank we were travelling.

'*Hahaha!*' the voice in my head had said. 'Of course I haven't done something so sensible and responsible, I didn't even know that was a thing!'

'Oh damn, I forgot all about it,' I'd replied in real life. 'Thanks for reminding me.'

The bit related to a hypothetical situation of a teacher spending his holidays in America and hitting up an inordinate number of liquor stores and strip clubs in LA and Vegas. I performed an act out of a phone call between the bank and an increasingly awkward teacher to discuss the irregular activity on his card. In the end, the teacher gets so embarrassed he hangs up. I debuted it in front of Stephen and he began with his usual assessment that it was 'long', with which I already concurred, but he agreed it had potential to be funny. I knew by now Stephen only describes something as potentially funny if he truly means it. He suggested ways to shorten it and recommended that I play down the strip club bits for the same reasons regarding likability. However, he conceded there could be a slight reference to it as long as it wasn't overdone. The reputable teacher acting so far out of character was what provided the embarrassment and gave the joke its impact.

'I've gotta give it up for my bank,' I tried again as an act out. 'They're really looking out for me. They rang me because they noticed some irregular activity on my credit card. They said, "Sir, over the past two weeks there's been over $2000 spent at liquor stores and strip clubs across the USA. Should we put an emergency block on it?" I said, "Oh my god, really? [feigning indignant surprise] Oh no!... That's... um... really?... oh no... that's, err..."' At that point I made eye contact with Stephen and in unison we said: 'We're good'.

Together we laughed in earnest. It was a wonderful moment between us and he strongly encouraged me to keep the bit for Friday night.

My routine was almost complete, and once again I marvelled at how much work can go into just five minutes of stand-up. I felt as though I'd gained so much from my time at the ACI and I was, perhaps for the first time, truly looking forward with confidence to getting up at the Gotham Club.

'One last thing,' advised Stephen, 'you need to slow up.' He explained that speaking too quickly and being afraid of silence was a very common problem for new comedians.

'Learning to slow up is one of the keys to moving up. It's huge. Gigantic. All sorts of positive things come from simply learning to slow up.' He explained how he had seen many comedians significantly advance their careers by mastering the art of simply slowing their act and being more relaxed with it.

'When you learn to slow up you become a bigger presence. You become more powerful without even saying anything. It's like saying "I have stuff to say and it's going to be fun so I'm not going to rush it". They get to know you more, they get to feel what you feel.'

I recalled Steve Hughes saying a similar thing about not being afraid of silence. These were profound words.

'Remember Ben, you're the only one in the light.'

Thursday was my last evening to relax in America, as tomorrow was the big show and I was flying home early the next day. My time in New York had elapsed way too quickly. I'd have loved to spend another few months there to further absorb the culture and hang out with some new comedian buddies in the city that truly never sleeps. It felt odd that not only would I be home by Monday, but standing in front of a class, attending to yard duties and sitting through curriculum meetings. Not to disparage my regular life, as I do love teaching, but to stretch this fantasy further was something I would have done without hesitation. I vowed to return one day.

I was grateful for another deeply fulfilling time in America and it was certainly going to end on a high. It was sad that Sarah wasn't there to join me at the Gotham Club, but she took a lot of satisfaction from my regular texts about how this had been the most incredible and life-changing present ever. I'd planned to call her from the top of the Empire State Building that night, but I was told it's never quite as romantic as it seems, with tourists packed in like sheep every night of the year. So I settled for the rooftop of my hotel, from which I still enjoyed a stunning view of the lights of the Upper Westside and the bridges across the Hudson River. It was heartening to hear Sarah's voice from the other side of the world as she wished me luck for the Gotham Club. It was lunchtime on Friday back home, and when I heard the bell at her school it reminded me of how far away I was, both geographically and mentally.

Before going downstairs, I inserted my earphones and enjoyed the inspiring views of New York City for one last time to Alicia Keys' *Empire State of Mind*, perhaps one of the most cliched yet tranquil things I've ever done.

Gotham Comedy Club was established in 1996 in Lower Manhattan and in 2006 moved into larger premises within the same district – a charming 1929 building with a narrow frontage and a comically outdated theatre sign with flashing light bulbs advertising each night's acts. Tonight we were promoted as the *ACI Alumni Show* and it felt special to be considered an alumnus after only four days. It would be easy to miss the club without this sign, as it appeared to be squeezed between two hotels on either side, but after traversing a narrow corridor painted in distinctive Gotham Yellow (a colour made famous by New York cabs), it opened into a more cavernous theatre space. The corridor was adorned with signed portraits of those who had performed on this stage, including Robin Williams, Jerry Seinfeld, Larry David, Roseanne Barr, Dave Chappelle, Dane Cook, Jim Gaffigan, Chris Rock and Rosie O'Donnell. When the young lady behind the ticket counter asked, 'Performer or guest?', it felt quite fraudulent responding 'performer'. But then, I had worked hard to be here, and I certainly wasn't here just to watch.

In our last group session that afternoon, Stephen had gone over some of his final tips and expectations for the show. At first he'd reminded us that we *are* the show. We were not warming the stage before the pros began, we were the reason people were buying tickets and coming out for the night. He'd also enforced practical tips such as to avoid wearing clothing with writing on it that could distract the audience – advice I hadn't heard before, but it made good sense. Luckily, the one clean T-shirt I had left was nice and plain. And he suggested having nothing in your pockets except a cue card.

'It's always ok to go to the cue card if you lose your place," he reassured us, which I took comfort from after my LA disappointment. 'In fact, you can even get a laugh from it. "My next joke's really funny… and in just a moment I'll tell you what it is."'

And just before dismissing us for the final time from the New Yorker Hotel, he had slipped in one last important piece of advice. One little rule he'd almost forgotten, but was thankful to remember just in time.

'Oh, and by the way… under no circumstances consume any alcohol before the show.'

Whaaat?

Was he serious? With a quick glance I'd made brief eye contact with Kevin, a comic from LA with whom I'd enjoyed a couple of beers just the day before, and the mutual concern on his face confirmed everything. Stephen had been uncompromising with all he'd instructed of us so far, with good reason, and this would be no different. I think I mouthed the word 'fuck' without consciously meaning to.

As you've probably noticed by now, I do enjoy a sociable drink. Rest assured, I drink responsibly and can certainly have just as much fun without alcohol. But the unfortunate thing for any comedian who is trying to be even a little conscious of booze consumption is that our favourite hobby takes place almost exclusively in licensed venues. Add to that pre-show nerves and a lot of waiting around, and before you know it a drink in the hand can become a goddamn ritual. And tonight was not a night I wanted to break any rituals. To make matters worse, performers were asked to sit at the bar while not on stage as it was out of the way. Patrons in American comedy clubs don't order drinks at the bar, only by table service. If you approach the bar for a drink you will appear rude and impatient, as I'd discovered by accident more than once. So our instruction for before and during the show was to sit at the bar and drink water if thirsty. As foreign as this felt, I trusted Stephen and, more to the point, I was way too scared to break any of his rules.

The audience seating at Gotham is the classic style of tightly packed round tables in front of the stage with a reddish curtain backdrop. A spotlight was already fixed on a microphone stand and stool, the latter of which was used by some comedians to sit, or place a drink. It felt so authentic, so true to the classic image of comedy clubs we've seen for years on TV. When Judd Jones, our MC, let us on stage to look out across the empty room, it occurred to me that I'd stood on plenty of comedy stages by now, but this was the first time it had felt the way I'd always pictured it. Judd ensured we all knew where the red light was at the back of the room. Our five-minute time limit would be strictly enforced. As professional shows in America run to a tight schedule, there would be no tolerance for sticky feet (he didn't actually say 'sticky feet' because as far as I know that's an Australian expression, but he was more than clear).

'When this light is on, you get off,' he directed. So far Judd had been jovial and great fun, but when discussing the red light he seemed to briefly channel a hot-headed drill sergeant. 'And if the light is flashing, it means I'm about to get on stage and rip the mic out of your hands.'

I think that neatly clarified the red light situation. But as I was normally precise with timing, I had no problem with it and wished this attitude would catch on in Melbourne.

'And remember,' Judd added, 'what's the most important thing of all? Ben?'

I was glad he chose me out of the group, because I guessed correctly. It was the last thing Stephen had told us this afternoon before we departed, and it was the best advice you could ever hear in comedy. After all of the workshops, feedback, hits, misses and analyses both at home and abroad, it was perhaps the best advice I've ever received.

'Have fun,' I said.

'Exactly. Enjoy the experience, everybody. Have a lot of fun up there tonight.'

Remembering this immediately eased my nerves. I recalled my first Brunny gig, and several since, when I had distinctly enjoyed the stage experience. That was my aim for tonight. Straight away I felt more relaxed, and under normal circumstances would have grabbed a drink from the bar.

When the doors opened, the audience filled quickly and the room became a bustle of activity as patrons arranged themselves at tables and serving staff plied them with drinks. We were told fifty-seven tickets had been pre-sold and that we could expect almost as many walk-ups, so a crowd of about 100 seated closely together soon formed. While the usual nerves kicked in, I observed I was becoming less perturbed by crowd sizes. At this point there was little difference between a crowd of fifteen or 150. Both will laugh if you're funny, and the silence from either is pretty much the same if you're not.

As Judd opened the show the room was immediately pretty warm. He got big early laughs and it seemed the punters were here to have a good time. That was never a guarantee of laughter of course, as I'd seen plenty of comedians pour cold water all over a warm room, but the audience was at least focused on the show, and with full table service people rarely left their seats.

Each of the first few comedians did a great job. It was so insightful to observe acts I'd seen workshopped all week hitting their mark in front of a real paying audience. So many great set-ups and punchlines appeared so natural, sometimes even spontaneous. If only the audience could have seen the toil that went into reworking them to the point of performance, they would be doubly impressed.

Joan was third on the bill. She spoke with great confidence, her experience as a preacher no doubt being of great value here, and delivered what was essentially one long anecdote punctuated with laughs. Her style was humorously self-deprecating as she spoke about the trials of being a preacher in an increasingly secular world, and the story culminated in her finding a park ranger arriving at a car park outside a church in a Wisconsin mountain range. He was getting ready to issue parking fines to every vehicle, when she enquired as to whether he had a relationship with Jesus. As other members of the congregation made their way towards the car armed with bibles and flyers, he spun his truck around and high-tailed it out of there faster than you could say 'Hallelujah!'. Joan linked this back to her original contention, highlighting there were some great advantages to being a pastor in modern society. It was extremely funny and well received, and I could see Stephen beaming as a proud mentor.

By the time Laura Bassi stepped up, about an hour into the show, the audience was thankfully still warm. They were having a great time and Laura got a big first laugh. But I remember little else of her act. Why? Because I was next. And suddenly I was thankful for Stephen's rules, as I was definitely feeling fresher than usual for the alcohol prohibition. Unlike many open mic nights in Melbourne pubs, this environment was certainly not one for a half-drunk comedian unless it was part of their schtick. Tonight was about precision. It was about hitting the right emphasis on words and remembering to pause for exactly the right amount of time. It was about slowing down your delivery at the same time as your heart was racing. It was about concentrating on every little detail while at the same time having lots of fun. Comedy can be a very serious funny business at times.

Judd introduced me and I stepped up to very encouraging applause, and as usual I was struck by the brightness of the lights. Something that is unnoticeable to audiences is that the comic is often blind on stage, and this was the most blind I've ever been. I literally couldn't see anybody. I was grateful that Judd didn't bring me on with the usual 'All the way from Australia...', as I feel it's the comedian's role to tell their own story, so I introduced myself as an Aussie and began with observations of the crappy American TV shows we were forced to endure back home.

I landed a couple of good laughs early and the tension of the week surged out of me. What followed was one of the most rehearsed sets I've ever done. I think I pretty much got all the words right and hit the right inflections and pauses as practised with Stephen, and that it looked natural enough. I was relieved to get strong laughs throughout, and in all the right places. As my enjoyment kicked in, I began to experience a strange sensation, as though I was thinking with two brains at once – one continued with the routine, while the other simultaneously absorbed the moment. I almost had to pinch myself that I was getting laughs at the Gotham Comedy Club, and loving it! Less than four years ago comedy was a distant dream, yet here I was, standing on one of the most famous stages in New York.

I finished my set to humbling applause, saying 'I've waited my whole life to say this: Thank you New York! You're a beautiful city!' As Stephen had advised, the cheers became even louder.

The post-show catch-up was delightful. Comedians were relieved after a week of nerves, and many punters stayed to chat. There was an enthusiasm to meet us here that I had never experienced in Australia. Almost every audience member I chatted to spoke glowingly of my act and asked how much longer I'd be in New York. Painfully, I responded each time with, 'Until tomorrow morning'. I didn't want to leave so soon, but I couldn't imagine a better memory to take out of my last night. I also wholeheartedly enjoyed chatting with Joan. Outside of this forum, an evangelical pastor from Wisconsin and an atheist from Down Under would probably have little in common, but here we were just two people with stories to tell and we both enjoy making others laugh. Maybe we weren't so different after all.

And it was fantastic to catch up with Stephen after the show.

'Well done, Ben,' he beamed, with a firm handshake and even firmer eye contact. 'Well done.'

On the flight home I listened to a lot of the audio recordings I'd made of Stephen's feedback in the group and private sessions, and transcribed as much as I could into another A4 exercise book. I also caught snippets of the feedback he'd given those who'd performed immediately before me as I'd normally start my recording early. At one point he was giving advice to a young comic about where to place the emphasis within her punchline.

'You have to really punch *dick*,' he explained, and I could clearly picture his businesslike straight face. 'Remember where the laugh is. Work backwards from dick.'

Work Backwards from Dick. I almost thought that could be the title of Stephen Rosenfield's book about comedy if he ever wrote one. I'm eternally grateful that it wasn't, as he authored a book that was published just weeks later titled *Mastering Stand-up*. For anyone interested in this wonderful but increasingly complex artform, it's one of the best reads you can find.

Now it was time to apply my new lease on comedic life to projects back home. I was hoping to start moving in some exciting new directions.

16

FRINGE

In the weeks after returning from America, I gave serious thought to what my next step in comedy might be. I was beginning to desire bigger challenges and I wanted to keep moving forward. At the same time, I was recalling the words of Khaled Khalafalla when he had questioned why producing my own Comedy Festival show had to be such a distant dream.

The Melbourne International Comedy Festival presently hosted more than 600 shows of varying production scale per year. At the top end were headline shows featuring local and overseas professionals, many of whom make much of their annual income from major festivals. The Melbourne Town Hall and large theatres in the city were popular venues for these. Then there were medium level shows, where you could see Evan Hocking's *The Morning After* or Tom Siegert as *The Suburban Footballer* at local venues. Sarah and I had taken a group of friends to see these two shows back-to-back at the Hotel Barkly in St Kilda the previous year, and it was one of the funniest nights we can remember. In addition, there are many smaller amateur productions spread around Melbourne. These might be solo comedians, small theatre companies putting on sketch or dramatic comedy, or a pair or group of comedians splitting a bill in a show that resembles what you'd see at a high-quality open mic night. Many of these are performed to small audiences that pay $10-20. I'd already attended plenty of small shows put on by people I knew. For instance, before Evan started selling out larger venues, one of his early festival shows was attended by Sarah and me and only four other people, and together we filled about a quarter of the tiny room opposite the Melbourne Town Hall (admittedly this was a Wednesday night in the middle of a long run). It was still a great night, and it was encouraging to see that it's ok to start small. This was beginning to seem like something I could now aim for.

Creating a festival show became my next goal in comedy. I didn't care to make any money from it. In fact, I'd be happy to make a loss for the experience. I'd just love to be able to prove to myself that I could do it, and that I could be a part of the world renowned MICF. It would be a showcase of the hard work I'd put in over the past four years.

It was probably too late to be aiming for the 2018 festival. Registrations were closing soon, and more to the point, I wanted time to develop material with my new understanding of comedy writing. The 2019 festival became an exciting new goal.

My first creative objective was to come up with a theme. The best solo shows typically have an overarching narrative or central theme as opposed to being just a bunch of random material cobbled together. Evan's show traced a two-week period of his younger days when he went on 'a bit of a bender' and made some expensive mistakes. Likewise, Tony Magnusson's excellent show *Confessions of a Call Centre Assassin* was based on his experiences working for a utility company and dealing with crazy customers.

So what could my narrative be? I'd led a reasonably interesting life so far, but interesting enough to sell tickets? I didn't know yet.

Could I talk about my life as a teacher? There's potential there, and it could attract a large target audience, but I knew of a similar festival show already being prepared by a small group of teachers so it might lack originality, and besides, I didn't like the idea of mixing comedy with my professional life. It's fine for a call centre operator dealing with irate customers every day, but in education there's a much greater duty of care, and my teaching career is my daytime passion. If I was to joke about my students (which would inevitably happen a lot) my biggest concern, as Stephen would point out, would be that the audience would *believe* me. And that's not the image I wanted for myself, as a comedian nor a teacher.

Another idea I considered was to expand upon my socially awkward routine and make it about 'growing up' as an adult, reaching your forties and realising life doesn't follow a script. I'd developed a growing awareness that a lot of people in midlife feel unhappy by comparing their lives to others, when really they should be proudly embracing their own stories, and having a bit of a laugh with them. This could make for a fascinating show. My favourite shows have always been those that carry a positive message and leave audiences thinking well beyond the laughter, in the style of Adam Hills' *Happyism*. It was certainly worthy of consideration, either for now or in the future.

Often, however, good ideas would come to me not during brainstorming efforts, but in random moments that could wake me at night. Such was the moment when it struck me that I truly did have a unique story that could *only* be told only by me. Excitedly, I got out of bed and started taking copious notes on the closest paper I could find, and sent Sarah an annoyingly late text message.

'Well what's the idea?' she texted back.

'Comedy Speed Dating the Stage Show. LOL xx', I replied.

'U woke me 4 that?'

'It's a great idea, believe me. We became experts on the dating scene. X'

I was perhaps using the word 'experts' a bit loosely, but I did feel as though our short-lived venture had given us great insight into the commercial dating world with some unexpected results. It had become an inadvertent social experiment. For instance, I'd been particularly fascinated by the difficulty of attracting men when I'd anticipated the opposite. There was so much to discuss with so much comic potential: from turning up to the same speed dating event as my ex, jokes about the single life, and trying to understand how this lack of male interest was in direct contrast to the peacocking behaviour of the nightclub scene. In essence, I had a show about human relationships, perhaps the most universal theme of all. It allowed for self-deprecation with observational and anecdotal humour, and had plenty of space for philosophical musings and leaving the audience with positive afterthoughts. I even considered running a quick speed dating event afterwards for willing audience members, maybe even as part of the act, to give my show a truly unique selling point.

The potential for a great show was huge, and it had been in front of me the whole time. Was this something I would realistically be able to achieve? With a new focus, I ploughed back into the open mic scene to workshop material. As a teacher, I've often found goal-setting the most effective way to re-engage students, and once again the same was proving just as effective for myself.

It was a wintry Tuesday when I found myself back where the whole journey had started — lying on my couch. The best open mic option on Tuesday was normally *Mad Dog*, but on this night the couch was winning the battle of wills. A lazy evening in tracksuit pants in front of the heater, with rain as a backdrop to the TV, was clearly more inviting than a long drive to the western suburbs just to do a five-minute spot, especially considering I would need to endure at least another two hours of amateur comedy on the most fucking uncomfortable wooden seats ever (I'm sorry but if the owners of this otherwise fine pub are reading this, come on!). Any lesser man or woman would have already had their ugg boots on by now, but I had a clear moment when my mind harked back to my very first comedy experience, and how if I hadn't pushed myself I would not have had any of the wonderful experiences I've enjoyed since then. So with my new goal and potential festival material to practise, I willed myself to get in the car and drive through the rain. And I'm certainly glad I did. I have since considered this to be the 'sliding door' moment that significantly impacted the next part of my journey, as it was on this bleak Tuesday night in August 2017 that I formally met Adam Jacobs.

I recognised Adam as a regular from the Lounge workshops, where he was one of the more accomplished amateur comedians considered good enough to perform on the main stage. He'd always been an enthusiastic contributor to workshops, bounding up on stage at any opportunity and offering constructive feedback to many others. Adam was a true student of comedy. As I was soon to discover, he had a vast knowledge of comedians of all eras. He would reference some I'd never heard of as though they were household names. When I recommended Stephen Rosenfield's book he immediately downloaded it, and I'm sure he would have consumed it within a couple of days. Adam's feedback on comedy was to become the most insightful and knowledgeable I'd ever experienced from another amateur, and when he got to know somebody he took pride in helping them with their craft. It's no wonder he's also a school teacher. But first, to say hello.

During a quiet moment soon after I'd performed, I took a rare chance to catch Adam on his own and introduced myself. He knew who I was and it was nice to chat for the first time. I'd always admired his work and figured we probably had a lot in common, as we were pretty much the same age and similar in style, but he certainly had a more well-defined and unique persona on stage. In addition, Adam wore a distinctive set of chops (sideburns) and sometimes a woollen flat cap. We chatted briefly about some upcoming gigs and lamented the demise of the Lounge workshops, and eventually I told him about my idea for a festival show.

'That sounds really interesting,' he said earnestly. 'So speed dating is kind of like the opposite of Tinder?'

'Yeah, I couldn't believe how hard it was to sell to blokes. The Tinders of the world have killed it – blokes prefer to swipe through hundreds of photos these days. Who wants to be stuck talking to the same person for six minutes?'

'That's way too long,' laughed Adam. He looked genuinely intrigued by my story. 'There's the premise for your show. Has Tinder killed speed dating? There are so many ways you could make that work. It's like you performed a social experiment.'

'I know,' I laughed. They were my words exactly.

'Good luck with it, mate,' he said. 'Keep in touch. It was great to chat.' We shook hands as he departed and I felt genuinely chuffed. Sometimes when an idea sounds good in your mind it can turn out to be a real dud in reality, but to hear this one validated by someone of Adam's experience was invigorating. After a few minutes I was about to leave, but then Adam returned.

'I was just thinking, do you want to try out some of your material at the Fringe?' he asked.

The Melbourne Fringe Festival was opening in a couple of weeks. A wonderful celebration of the arts, the Fringe was open to all disciplines, and comedy had become a common one in recent years.

'For sure,' I replied. 'How would I do that? It's a bit late, isn't it?'

'No, I've got a spot booked for three nights at the Highlander Bar. It's forty-five minutes, I was using it to prepare for next year's Comedy Festival, but why don't we split it? Do half the time each, you can give your material a run and see what it needs.'

'Oh wow. Um... yeah, that would be great,' I stammered. 'But I wasn't really aiming for next year's festival.'

'Why not? See how it goes, I reckon your idea's a good one.'

It was an exciting offer, one that I never considered turning down, because to perform at any type of festival at the moment would be the challenge I craved. Also, this would be a more natural progression than going straight to the MICF. As Adam pointed out, it would be a great way to get a genuine read of my material, as a show format can be very different to open mic. The only problem for me was the maths. Half of 45 minutes, I'm pretty sure, is 22.5. And I'd just demonstrated how much work can go into perfecting just a five-minute routine at the Gotham Club. This would take a lot of intense preparation.

'Sounds great, I'd love to do it,' I confirmed. 'When's the spot?'

'In three weeks.'

Highlander Bar is located in a laneway off Flinders Street, one of Melbourne's busiest roads, yet I'd never heard of it before. This great city has a lot of hidden gems, and I immediately grew to love this cosy pub and its Scottish theme. The small upstairs function room was perfect for a small comedy show, with seating for about forty people spread across couches and a ring of folded chairs. There was a professional PA system and lighting, but no elevated stage, which created a nice sense of intimacy. Importantly, there was no upstairs bar in use, so the lack of foot traffic suited performers. As the venue of my upcoming first festival contribution, I was pretty happy with it. Its oddity was the painted-on fireplace behind the performance area and other random images on the walls, including a bear posing for a sepia style photograph wearing a suit and hat. It wasn't a fun-loving bear like Humphrey, it just sat with a solemn expression in the way people did in the olden days before it was commonly agreed that we could smile for photos. It was a little distracting to have such a busy wall behind the stage, but overall its quirkiness gave this space the perfect feel for a comedy room.

Adam ran an open mic session here every Wednesday known as *Comedy at Highlander,* which I promptly attended the following night. It was a nice, tight one hour show that finished strictly on time at the relatively early hour of 8pm, and many comics would then leave to do sets elsewhere. I loved this efficiency. It was a very performer-friendly bar and I enjoyed my first spot the following week. However, another distraction was the mirrored wall behind the audience. It was rather unusual to see yourself on stage, and I learnt to avoid looking. If a joke fell flat you could almost feel sorry for the awkward looking bloke staring back at you.

With limited time to prepare for the Fringe I began writing immediately, using the technique encouraged by Stephen to write routines word-for-word, underlining the laughs. I was now finding this quite useful, especially for trimming the fat. I was identifying laughs and getting to them as quickly as practical. However, as I'd discovered in New York, one of the 'drawbacks' of being concise is that it makes your set shorter. And when you're trying to compose a 22.5 minute set for the first time, every minute of reliable material is gold. Over several days, I wrote my proverbial butt off.

Adam created some last-minute social media advertising, calling our show *Adam and Ben – Has Tinder Killed Speed Dating?* If we'd had a better think-tank session around one of the barrels at Highlander I'm sure we'd have come up with a catchier title, but it did the job for now. I was more than happy for just friends and family to come along, plus any walk-up crowd from the downstairs bar, as there were still many people in my life who had never seen me perform, and doing an official show as opposed to a five-minute spot was a much better way to invite them into this new world of mine. But Adam was quite into promotion, reiterating that comedy can be a serious business. Even though our show was free, we had to remunerate the venue owner by doing our best to bring people to their bar. So we did plenty of work in the short time we had to promote online and through word of mouth.

I presumed I'd be the first act. I'd open the show with my new routine before introducing Adam, the more accomplished comedian, as the headliner.

'Nah mate,' he said. 'You're the main act – you're going second. Let me know how much time you need and I'll make sure I bring you out on time. Just enjoy it.'

On paper, my routine was coming along pretty well. I was planning to open with some regular material before reflecting upon the single life and online dating experiences, which would shift nicely into the story of seeing my ex at the speed dating event, being refused a refund and launching my own business. In doing so, I would ponder the nature of dating in the modern age, and with a tinge of sadness question whether the Tinder culture was killing not just speed dating, but the basic human quality of bonding through laughter first.

I was very happy with it. Now I just needed to remember it, so I practised like never before.

Our three spots were booked for a Monday, Tuesday and Friday night in early September. The start of spring was a great time for people to be going out for a night of laughs. And as Friday would clearly attract the biggest audience, this gave us a chance to gauge our show earlier in the week and patch over any cracks.

In the days before our opening night, my only major concern was that my routine didn't have a strong opener. There's a saying in comedy that you should always finish on your funniest joke and open with your second funniest. But I really just wanted to open with some audience interaction, as it was a skill I was still developing to establish being in the room, even if I was mostly relying on practised spontaneity. I'd planned on asking people what they were drinking and whether they'd ever tried to cut back on the booze, leading into some material about my own failed attempts to do so. It was tested and reliable. However, in a setting like this, the opening still needed a belly laugh.

Enter Pauline Hanson.

For those too young to remember the controversial senator before she became a contestant on *Dancing with the Stars*, Pauline Hanson was often outspoken on social and racial issues and could attract widespread condemnation, even before the age of social media. I can only believe I'd done something to appease some kind of god (perhaps Joan had my back) when, in the days leading up to our opening night, Hanson rocketed back into the headlines by turning up to Federal Parliament wearing a full-length burqa protesting against the rights of Muslim women to do so in public. The mainstream media was outraged and screamed headlines of racism for a couple of days. That was the only window I needed. From that moment, my opening pretty much wrote itself.

'I didn't even want to quit drinking,' I complained to the audience on Monday night. 'I just told my girlfriend I'd quit drinking the day Pauline Hanson wears a burqa!'

The line landed perfectly. Only eight people were in attendance, but a *big* laugh from all of them instantly hooked them into the show and sent my confidence soaring. The value of a big early laugh can never be underestimated, for audience and performer alike. And I'd never been so grateful for Pauline Hanson. I was particularly pleased, as apart from five punters who we'd managed to lure upstairs from the main bar as they clearly had nothing better to do on a Monday, the rest of the audience consisted of Matthew, his partner Emily and his good mate Blaise.

As my narrative veered through my very short-lived attempt at finding love through speed dating and my subsequent business venture, it was received with very pleasing reactions in all the right places. By now I had grown a sharp ear to the difference between genuine laughter and the obligatory laughter that might be heard from family and friends, or a small audience that may force a laugh to give the comedian feedback. This was real laughter, the type where people look for eye contact with friends in order to share the moment. The type that tells the comedian they are in control of the room and the audience is hanging on your next word, trusting you to be funny and letting down their critical guard. It might have been a small crowd, but it was an honest one. And I was exhilarated to get through more than twenty minutes of material remembering everything perfectly, continuing to exorcise the demons of LA. I'd even involved a new prop for the climax. As I told the story of the rude customer service from the speed dating company that banned me, and angrily hypothesised how one day I might start my own that was going to be much better and focus more on laughter, I unravelled the two-metre banner left over from our business, featuring a pair of bright yellow smiling emojis in love, and proudly declared 'Comedy Speed Dating!' to rapturous applause. I then reflected upon the social experiment. I couldn't have been happier with the way it finished, leaving the audience with a positive message about the importance of bonding through laughter first.

Adam was stoked, and reiterated that I definitely had the basis of a solid festival show. We discussed a couple of bits to smooth over for the following night, but overall there was nothing major to address.

Relaxing with Matthew, Emily and Blaise after the show was a wonderful relief, and I was glad for Matthew to have seen probably my best effort to date. Having been there since my disastrous debut at Station 59 four years ago, he of all people could appreciate my journey. For the first time I think he looked genuinely proud of his dad as a comedian rather than just somebody who had the guts to try it. And I was grateful for the chance to socialise with them all. It reinforced to me how comedy nights can be such a naturally fun way to bring people together.

The following night I was thankful that Sarah could make it, as she was the other person who deserved to see this. Unfortunately, the bar was a lot quieter on Tuesday, so by the time the show started she was still the entire audience. Undeterred, Adam started anyway, as it's customary for festival shows to go ahead with small audiences – even *no* audience – as punters will often wander in when they hear something happening. If nothing else, conceded Adam, it would be a good dress rehearsal for some minor improvements before our anticipated big night on Friday, and even one person paying attention can make a massive difference to performing in front of empty chairs. I was disappointed for Sarah that she wouldn't get the proper experience of hearing laughter, but she'd become objective enough by now to recognise improvements to my work. By the time Adam finished there was still only one seat occupied, and Sarah welcomed me on to stage with a charitable clap. I began my 'crowd work' by asking her what she was drinking.

'Coke, honey,' she replied. 'You just bought it for me because I'm driving you home tonight.'

'Aww, thanks.'

Adam politely excused himself to leave for another gig and I continued my rehearsal for Sarah. It progressed well and she chuckled at some of the new bits, and this time I utilised the mirror on the back wall to observe myself, which was weird, but helpful. Thankfully, a second audience member soon joined us – a heavy-set businessman who settled comfortably into an armchair. I greeted him warmly and carried on with renewed vigour, pleased that my audience now outnumbered me. I don't remember him laughing much, except for a couple of smirks as he sipped on his beer, stretching out with his shoes off as though at home in front of the TV. At the end of the show he applauded generously, and I thanked him for coming and asked if he had enjoyed the show.

'Yes, thank you,' he replied. 'If you could help me, I was actually looking for the toilet?'

Friday night was a completely different caper. As it nicely coincided with the last day of the school term, many friends from work turned up, most of whom were in a very relaxed mood, slightly liquored up and primed for laughter. I also had some personal friends make the effort, including Drew and Sarah, a couple I have been great mates with for many years, and Tony Magnusson, who I was thrilled to see settling into the armchair occupied by the large businessman three nights earlier. Several punters had also made their way up from the main bar. The usual nervous jitters were appearing, and while so much of Stephen's advice since New York was continuing to assist me, I must admit I'd had a couple of drinks by now to calm them.

In all there were probably thirty people in attendance. I was thrilled by this, and in this intimate space it felt like a much larger crowd. It struck me that this was now the biggest gig of my life to date, even bigger than the Gotham Club. Not in terms of numbers, or occasion, but for the first time most of these people had come to see *me*. I was not one of many performers, I was the main act with my name alongside Adam's on the chalkboard downstairs. Most of this audience had planned their whole evenings around this, and I now had the potential to ruin them all. My heart raced, so I closed my eyes for a moment and remembered Stephen's best advice – to 'Just have a lot of fun up there tonight'.

'I'll get off now because you've all come to see one man haven't you,' conceded Adam with a laugh. 'Please welcome him onto the stage, give it up for Ben Tiffen!'

I stepped up to probably my most rousing applause yet from an enthusiastic, slightly drunk and mostly familiar crowd, and began with some interesting discussion of drinking choices, this being the last day of term. Of course, my good mate Aaron decided to engage with me about football, which threw me a little as I still didn't like departing too much from my script, but I was grateful for the interaction. Thankfully, the Pauline Hanson bit landed well again, and it launched what was without doubt the most fun experience I've ever had on the comedy stage. Every punchline just seemed to hit and the audience was there to laugh: I even heard a couple of endearing nose snorts. During my act I thought back to the Brunny and realised this was a similar experience on a much grander scale. I was also developing a consciousness of 'joyous communication' – a mindset explained by Stephen that does not mean being joyful all the time, but rather being excited to have the opportunity to express your emotions, whether that be joy, misery or frustration. Once I'd been made aware of this, I began to notice how passionate the best comedians were about whatever they were saying, and how joyous they were to share it. I'd been making an effort to do the same and I could feel it helping me perform tonight.

By the end of the show I was elated. The audience had lapped it up and, finally, my whole journey into comedy seemed to be making sense. I'd provided an event, a fun night out for many, and told them a story only I could tell. Tonight I'd been a host and entertainer. It was by far my favourite moment of this crazy journey so far.

Later in the evening, among a lot of warm congratulations and continued festivities for the start of school holidays (I'm sure teachers appreciate them even more than students do), I stole a moment of quiet reflection with Adam. He'd become a good mate in a short time, and I particularly valued his feedback. He said that he genuinely loved it and thought I had a solid premise for a full show. He pointed out that including audience banter, I'd done almost half an hour. A good festival show, he reminded me, is normally around forty minutes, with an additional support act to stretch it out. I was almost there already.

'Why don't you aim for next year's festival?' he suggested. 'Registrations are still open for 2018. There's no point waiting another year just to add ten more minutes.'

For the first time I began to give this serious consideration. I'd pushed myself hard over the past three weeks and delivered a product that worked. And it was already three quarters of all I needed for an MICF show. Perhaps I could do this. Perhaps I could see myself in the glossy *Herald Sun* festival guide in just over six months. Perhaps this was the moment for my comedy journey to peak, one that had taken me from Richmond to LA, London, New York, Footscray and now a Scottish bar in the city. It was an exhilarating prospect and I resolved to give it a go.

I was going to produce a show for the Melbourne International Comedy Festival in 2018.

'Good on you, mate,' reassured Adam. 'How hard can it be?'

17

FULL CIRCLE

Of the many things to organise when planning a Comedy Festival show, one of the most important is the venue. Simply finding an available stage with lights and a PA system is not enough. The venue as a whole, including its location, needs to be suitable for paying customers to have a fun and convenient night out. The MICF offered its own festival managed venues, but competition for these was strong so many comedians would find their own. A good pub in the inner suburbs with a performance space and a lively atmosphere was what I needed. Highlander Bar would have been perfect, but was already fully booked. Other similar bars were offering spots for festival shows, but most were also fully booked or not appealing. Having left my planning relatively late, I was finding this difficult. Perhaps my best chance was to simply go to an area that I liked and scope for a potentially untapped venue. From Comedy Speed Dating, I learned that venue owners are often keen for anything that will bring a crowd, so I decided to make my own luck. I started in Brunswick Street, Fitzroy – a traditionally bohemian area and one of my favourites. It was active on the comedy scene and had a lot of lively bars that might suit.

By sheer chance, I stuck my head inside a bar that seemed to have some upstairs renovations in progress and said hello to the owner, who explained he was building a new function room with a fully equipped stage. It would be completed by January and he had always been keen to get involved with the Comedy Festival. It was a perfect match! We talked turkey and shook hands, and I couldn't believe my luck.

With a venue secured, I could now turn my focus towards the most important element – preparing my act. For the next month or so I ran old and new material through the open mic scene, before eventually taking some time off to relax as usual at Venus Bay over the Christmas break, and then Sarah and I drove to Eagle Point – a serene coastal town in eastern Victoria. Feeling refreshed upon returning to Melbourne, I rang my venue to confirm the progress of their renovations. There was no answer, so I tried a few more times throughout the day and evening with the same result. Perhaps they were not working over the New Year period. No drama, I thought, and shot the owner an email to touch base. After a few more days, a couple more emails and several more unanswered phone calls, I was growing increasingly anxious. I drove back to Brunswick Street to find dusty delivery boxes waiting by the venue's door and many days' worth of uncollected mail stuffed into the slot. This was not looking good!

Eventually I resorted to contacting the owner through Facebook, of all things, and he humbly explained that his business was struggling due to lack of finance. The renovations were on hold indefinitely and they wouldn't be able to host my show. I explained in no uncertain terms that it would have been nice for him to contact me as soon as he was aware of this, as it was now January and I had no venue. I was screwed!

I placed a frantic call to the festival organisers, who were sympathetic and allowed me a maximum of three weeks to secure another venue before the absolute cut-off date, otherwise my dream would be on hold for another year. I'd come too far now to let that happen, so I sent a distress signal to as many venues as I could by scrutinising last year's festival guide and emailing almost every appropriate venue in it. Understandably, I did not get much positive response. With so many shows already registered, pretty much all venues had filled their allotted spots and begun their promotions. I was about to give up. But then I received one response that was different.

It was a phone number and four simple words: 'Call me. Paul Blackburn.'

Paul was the owner of St Kilda Comedy Club. At first I wondered why I'd never been to St Kilda Comedy Club, but I was soon to learn that it was not a building, it was Paul's business that would produce festival shows, small events and open mics nights in various parts of St Kilda. When I explained my situation, he invited me for a chat at the new bar he'd just opened in Blessington Street. It was not far from the National Theatre where I'd loved studying drama as a child, and driving past it the next day I was filled with a sense of nostalgia; it's one of the few buildings from my childhood that remarkably looks no different today. It struck me that if I was to perform my show in St Kilda it would be a nicely rounded journey. A full circle. I'd be returning to where my love of performing began.

Paul Blackburn was a similar age to me, about my height but lankier, and wore a Trilby hat that I was soon to discover rarely left his head. It was a sunny afternoon as I greeted him at his newly opened bar, a tiny wedge of a venue with no exterior walls and mostly street seating. He struck me immediately as an astute businessman, but with a casual air that was immediately likeable. I would come to observe that he would often complain about being under the pump, yet by contrast remain perpetually chilled. We began by having a good chat about comedy, and life.

I was looking for a venue, but Paul was looking for a show to produce. He explained that he already had two shows in production under the banner of St Kilda Comedy Club. One was for Nikki Osborne – an actress who I'd seen recently on *Hoges*, the biographical Paul Hogan mini-series (later she would appear on *I'm a Celebrity Get Me Out of Here* and was responsible for dressing former footballer Billy Brownless in a mankini for a charity photoshoot – thanks Nikki!). The other was a double act featuring Vince Sorrenti and Elliot Goblet. This was now sounding ridiculous! I felt as though we were at cross purposes; I explained to Paul that there was a slight misunderstanding and thanked him for his time. But he didn't want to end the conversation. His bar was holding an official opening with a comedy night the following Tuesday and he wanted me to be involved. He explained there would be some accomplished comedians there, including local St Kilda identities such as C.J Fortuna and Andrew Goodone, who I'd seen in the past and greatly admired, and he was interested in getting me up in front of them. I sensed he was on board with treating me as a 'prospect', as though he would like to unearth a new talent to work with alongside much more experienced comics, the likes of which I'd enjoyed since watching *Hey Hey it's Saturday* as a kid.

I was simultaneously thrilled and completely freaked out.

I turned up the following Tuesday at least as nervous as I'd been for any of my previous big events, including the Gotham

Club. It was an interesting venue with a small performance area crammed into a corner with most of the audience seated on the footpath beneath resplendent elm trees. Comedy al fresco. Before the gig I was introduced to C.J Fortuna; perhaps slightly older than me, he was a regular of the St Kilda comedy scene and a hardened pro. As the MC for the evening he greeted me warmly and explained that Paul had instructed him to check me out, which added to my nerves, but he wished me well and was great to talk to.

The show began with the fading sun to an audience of about thirty-five or so, spread out between the venue and street seating. I was relieved for a smaller crowd than I was expecting, but anxious because performers were standing very much in the audience's space. It invited much more interaction, which to be honest still wasn't my strength. Uniquely, members of the public would pass between the stage and the audience, often walking dogs or pushing prams, so when delivering punchlines about oral sex with a vegan I now had to consider whether a family was strolling by. But it did provide an interesting new dynamic and a chance to interact with willing members of the public.

Fortunately, my set went well. The audience was in a good mood and gave me plenty of laughs (as did a couple of people collecting laundry from across the street), and I was relieved to get a hearty ovation. It was an enjoyable gig, and I'd proven myself to Paul and some more experienced comedians who had been laughing in earnest. As soon as Paul was able to take time out from behind the bar he gave me a big, sweaty hug.

'That was awesome, man,' he said. 'You're definitely going to perform for St Kilda Comedy Club. I'm going to produce your festival show!'

So that was it. Paul now had three shows in production for the 2018 Melbourne International Comedy Festival: a double act featuring Vince Sorrenti and Elliot Goblet, Nikki Osborne's debut comedy show *On the Spectrum*, and me. It felt surreal that he had agreed to this, but having performed for him successfully at an important event he was willing to take a punt. For a moment I definitely had some doubts. I did suddenly feel out of my depth, and the worst thing I could do at this stage was overreach and let Paul down. But I reminded myself that for every step of this journey, from my nervous debut at Station 59, to the Gotham Club in New York and then the Fringe Festival, I had pushed myself. This was an extraordinary opportunity, one that so many other comedians would give anything for. I would be crazy not to embrace it. I thanked him profusely and became an immediate and eternally grateful member of St Kilda Comedy Club.

Annoyingly, I still needed a name for my show, something short and catchy that reflected its main theme. A good pun always helps too. Adam Jacob's show *Best Daze of my Life* was about his journey into middle age as a teacher and comedian, stumbling through 'my midlife strife that manifests itself on my face as a pair of really dodgy sideburns'. The first time I'd seen Evan do a solo show he'd called it *Evan is a Place on Earth*. He was gifted with a name that rhymes well. Rhyming with my name was more difficult. Ben was too plain, and Tiffen sounded like nothing except 'stiffen', as I was constantly reminded by Microsoft spell checks. By sheer chance, however, I heard an AC/DC song on the radio at around the same time – a catchy song titled *Stiff Upper Lip*. Maybe there was pun potential after all. Most of my show was about struggling through the grind of life: trying to quit drinking, online dating, and starting a business that technically failed while learning a lot about the modern singles scene. The whole theme of my show was really about trying to persevere through it all while keeping a stiff upper lip. My festival show *Tiff Upper Lip* was born.

Paul liked the name, and the AC/DC song was going to be great as my walk-on music. All three of Paul's shows were now booked for Kingston City Hall (formerly Moorabin Town Hall), a short drive from St Kilda. Coincidentally, this venue had hosted an AC/DC concert in 1975. Obviously, I wouldn't be performing on the same stage as Bon Scott, as there were some much smaller performance spaces available, but it was a nice connection.

Paul sent me to Acland Street for a shoot with his photographer, Tim Barnett. I soon appreciated that comedian profile shots were probably some of the weirdest assignments for portrait photographers. 'Now raise one eyebrow,' Tim would instruct. 'Look confused. Look cynical. Tilt your head sideways, look at the camera, raise both eyebrows and smile on one side of your mouth.' I was doing more facial gymnastics than Mr Bean. Ultimately, my posters and flyers featured me wearing my standard black T-shirt with arms folded, looking down the camera with an expression that was halfway between cynical and hopelessly confused. By that stage, I was achieving the confused look pretty easily. Seeing myself on promotional posters and flyers was at first surreal (and work colleagues thought doubly so when they appeared in our staffroom), but it solidified to me that this was now official. To see my image in print alongside the logos of both the MICF and St Kilda Comedy Club reminded me that I'd arrived on a stage that was, well, still not big, but at least the next one up from wherever I was.

Now it was time to prepare material like never before. As much as Paul had been generous by speculating on me, and as much as I was enjoying his company as a new friend and mentor, he would remind me that I was representing his brand and putting on a show at the Melbourne International Comedy Festival. Anything less than my best possible effort would not be acceptable.

Over the next few weeks I ploughed through open mic opportunities. Leading into the festival is the hardest time to get good spots as everyone seems to be demanding stage time, but I was lucky enough to perform at Highlander most Wednesdays thanks to Adam, and a couple of other venues that offered short spots along the way. At one stage I had a juicy spot booked for the Brunny, but a couple of days beforehand a car ran over a fire hydrant and flooded the venue, resulting in the pub closing for lengthy renovations. (Sadly, *Funny at the Brunny* never returned, but to the credit of Glen Zen, roughly a year later he contacted everyone on the set list that night to perform at the opening of his new event down the road: *Funny Near the Brunny*. I was stoked to open the show on this inaugural night.) But overwhelmingly, my devotion was to St Kilda Comedy Club every Tuesday. The timing wasn't convenient; by this stage I was also very busy as the head of my school's English department, and even though I'm certain my professional life was never compromised by my comedy, balancing two highly demanding roles was becoming a challenge. I had to give up a lot of 'me' time to get everything done.

Overall, I was enjoying the unique atmosphere of the Blessington Street bar. The mostly outdoor environment, on a picturesque St Kilda streetscape, was much more relaxed than regular comedy venues. And I was feeling a spiritual reconnection to St Kilda, a vibrant suburb known for its art and music, and a subculture like no other in Melbourne. I've always loved this place. For some people, St Kilda is in their blood, and it was hard to imagine them living anywhere else. Paul and CJ might well have been examples of this. And I was getting to know other regulars of St Kilda Comedy Club, feeling more and more like a part of the family. I befriended Abhishek Panchal, a young Indian comedian new to Melbourne, and the extremely funny Pete Murphy, a top bloke with a great storytelling style. Keren Storai was a brilliant new comedian in her thirties whose persona as a self-deprecating alcoholic was so convincing it took me at least three gigs to realise she was putting it on (at least I think she was). Likewise, Billy Stiles was probably the funniest amateur going around. He never took too long to get to a punchline and in real life didn't differ too much from the lackadaisical character we saw on stage. I was also befriending professionals; Bev Killick is a highly regarded comedian and actor who I'd seen at the Comic's Lounge and on TV. The night I first met her at Blessington Street we sat and talked for more than an hour after the show. It's rare that I could meet someone new and talk for that long after such a long day of work and comedy, but I was thoroughly engaged in everything she told me about her life in the industry, including dream jobs on cruise ships and operations to entertain Aussie troops in the Middle East. The places comedy can take a person! I drove her home that evening and as she got out of my car at her St Kilda apartment, she asked, 'So are you addicted to comedy yet?'

I thought about this for a second and replied ambiguously, 'I think I'm getting there.'

'You will be,' she said, with a gleam in her eye. It was the gleam of a true addict.

Not long after that, Bev appeared in a TV commercial for Mars bars in which she played a life model who disrobes in an art class, embarrassing her son who is a student in the class. The first time I saw this image of a naked woman advertising chocolate bars, I was with friends, and I'm not sure they believed my sudden proclamation that 'she was just in my car!'

Another night while performing at Blessington Street, a rather large crowd formed throughout my set. 'How well am I going?' I thought to myself as almost every passer-by stopped to watch, and patrons began coming out from the restaurant next door to see what all the excitement was about. My heart flourished and I thought I'd ride this sudden wave of popularity and stay on stage for as long as I could, until I turned to see Dave Hughes waiting on deck. Hughesy lived locally and would sometimes pop in for a surprise performance. Suddenly realising that the large crowd was in fact just waiting for me to finish, I decided against an encore.

It was fun to chat to Hughesy again, who remembered me when I mentioned Comedy Speed Dating. We crossed paths a few more times in St Kilda. Even the best in Australia need a place to practise their material, and it was always a nice surprise when the big names turned up.

One night I was particularly excited to hear that Elliot Goblet would be performing. My deadpan comedy idol from *Hey Hey it's Saturday,* and now my St Kilda stablemate. When I nervously approached him, he was immediately affable. It was strange to hear him out of character (although his natural voice still has inklings of his signature monotone), and he introduced himself by his real name, Jack Levi. Over the next few weeks

I would get to know Jack, and I can genuinely say he is one of the nicest people I've met in comedy. He took a true interest in my journey and we chatted for quite a while as I told him about my American experiences and he talked about his early television gigs. He was delighted to help promote my show, as I was for his. The other half of his festival show, Vince Sorrenti, turned up the following week. Another from the *Hey Hey* class of comedians that I've loved since the 1980s, Vince is today one of Australia's highest earning comedians, performing mostly at well-paying corporate gigs. As I was introduced to Vince I thanked him for all the great laughs and told him that one of my all-time favourite bits was his old Kraft cheese routine. Without hesitation he broke straight into character, rubbing his tummy and saying, 'Mmm, those single slices wrapped in plastic are sooo nice. I'll have mine extra mild thanks, don't want to taste any of that cheese shit.' Like cheese on toast, I practically melted.

On the same night I also met Nikki Osborne, who was feeling nervous about debuting as a comedian. She was primarily an actor and model, and her show *On the Spectrum* was a combination of stand-up, storytelling, videos, and even some dancing. She ran short sections of her show through the Blessington Street open mic and it was received with great laughter. Unfortunately, her social media pages had already begun to be inundated with negativity regarding her choice to do a festival show about autism. While it was considered by some to be in poor taste, from what I could gather so far, her narrative was intended to be more about celebrating the unique attributes of her son and told in a loving way. It sounded exactly like what Stephen Rosenfield would have endorsed. Of course, the critics were happy to cut her down without having seen her show. I tried to reassure her that all would be fine once the show actually opened and people could see it for themselves, but still, it was a great cause of concern for Nikki and Paul.

Excitingly, Nikki invited me to take part in a short film she was producing as part of her act. *Escape to the Cuntry* was a parody of a small town in which political incorrectness was a celebrated flaw. My role was described as a seedy, misogynistic barman named Brett (Paul had told Nikki I'd be perfect for the role, for reasons I'm still slightly concerned about). We filmed in a day at St Kilda Sports Club, where I was reunited with John Burgos, who played a terrorist. It was heaps of fun and so great to act in a film – another childhood ambition that got lost along the way. I was beginning to live some of the great experiences that comedy can lead to. Sadly however, Nikki never completed the project, deciding that it didn't really fit her show as desired, and I never got to see myself on the big screen.

I did, however, make it onto the toilet wall. One night at Blessington Street while I was waiting for my set, I noticed two ladies sitting nearby who were scrutinising me as though they recognised me from somewhere but couldn't quite place it. I said hello and they told me that I looked very familiar. When I introduced myself by name they figured it out. Sadly, I realised I was not becoming famous. Paul had placed promotional posters for his shows around the bar, including the toilets, where apparently I'd been watching them wash their hands. But I was happy for any publicity. Paul had scheduled five shows for me at Kingston City Hall. I was planning on just three, like my Fringe run, and was concerned that five shows would be thinning out my audience. But Paul backed me to get some good promotion on the back of Elliot, Vince and Nikki, so I nervously agreed, and once again decided to take advantage of an amazing opportunity.

On the Saturday night before the festival started, I did some flyering around the Melbourne Town Hall, the hub of the festival. Many comics were out doing the same, and it became a wonderful catch up with many friends old and new, including Tim Young from Ballarat, who by now was also doing his own show. I brought flyers for all three of Paul's events, as I was happy to help out St Kilda Comedy Club as much as possible. I did feel a bit uneasy about approaching members of the public with flyers, as I normally detest that form of marketing, but it was a festive atmosphere and I reminded myself that I wasn't selling mobile phone plans. As it turns out, comedy can be a fun product to spruce. I asked people where they were from, and if they lived anywhere near Moorabin I would go for the hard sell. I also found that loitering around my own poster was a handy strategy. I could only presume a degree of randomness when the festival organisers placed their posters, as one of mine ended up in a prominent position directly beside Peter Hellier and Tom Gleeson! I felt more comfortable on the toilet wall. I can't imagine how many people walked past this combination thinking 'Who the hell is that guy?'. So if anyone stopped for a prolonged look I took the opportunity to surprise them and introduce myself, shoving a flyer in their hand and letting them know that my show was all about how to stay positive and keep a stiff upper lip. This was generally well received. I promoted the other shows as well and worked hard for St Kilda Comedy Club in recognition of the faith Paul had shown in me. I think I accidentally offended one man by suggesting he looked old enough to remember Elliot Goblet. When I told Jack Levi of this a few days later he couldn't stop laughing.

Paul had arranged for Elliot and Vince to perform over the first two weeks of the festival, followed by Nikki and myself in the latter half. This suited me, as my first two shows would take place within the school holidays. We had secured the ballroom area at Kingston City Hall, with a professional stage and plenty of seating on round tables in a similar manner to the Gotham Club (however the tables here were a bit larger and further apart). For the first night of Elliot and Vince, I turned up to watch and was promptly asked by Paul if I wouldn't mind being the announcer.

'Absolutely,' I replied without hesitation. It was a small contribution, but to be an official part of a show featuring Elliot and Vince was like a fantasy come true. My role would be to welcome the audience with the off-stage microphone and announce the MC, Brad Oakes, on stage at the beginning of the show and again after the interval. It sounded like a simple job, but this small role was now giving me something to feel nervous about. I was thrilled to be a part of the show, but as the first voice to be heard there was now pressure to perform at a professional level. I was working with three of Australia's best comedians, and this large paying audience would expect a faultless performance from everybody, including the inconspicuous announcer. And to think I'd only turned up to watch! I reminded myself that I'd never really paid attention to the performance of an announcer before, and nobody else would tonight. Unless, of course, I completely fucked it up.

Brad Oakes is a true professional, and when I practised my first announcement, thinking I'd done a pretty good job, he let me know otherwise. My role was much more than to simply introduce him, he explained, I had to work the audience up into an excitable state. They had to be ready to laugh as soon as a performer walked on stage. So when the audience was admitted, and we could hear the increasing hum of conversation that mirrored my increasing heart rate, Brad stood beside me. As Paul pumped up the intro music, Brad stood poised like an orchestra conductor waiting to bring me in. After just enough music, his finger dropped and for the next few seconds I was the invisible centre of attention.

'Ladies and gentlemen,' I boomed, in roughly the same manner as a WWE ringside announcer, 'Welcome to Kingston City Hall, where St Kilda Comedy Club presents an Evening with Elliot Goblet and Vince Sorrenti.' [Pause for cheers.] 'Are you ready to have a good time?'

There was a good response from the audience who were clearly here to have some fun, but Brad waved his arm in an 'up, up, up!' manner.

'I said... are you ready to have a good time?'

The audience cheered with more gusto, and Brad gave me a thumbs up.

'Then please put your hands together and welcome to the stage your MC for the evening... give it up for Braaad Oooakes!'

Brad ripped straight into material that immediately got great laughs. I relaxed, feeling an overwhelming sense of relief. Who would have thought something as simple as announcing an MC could be such an involved task? It reiterated to me how professional this industry can be.

Over the next three nights I revelled in my role as a twice-per-night announcer, taking great pride in each performance and in being a willing dogsbody for three of my favourite comedians. As performers don't like to be seen off-stage until after the show, I had no problem fetching drinks, chairs and whatever else for them, often using my unofficial status to say hello to their recognisable friends who had dropped in, such as Trevor Marmalade and Wilbur Wilde, chatting about *Hey Hey* to a point that probably annoyed them. But overwhelmingly, my biggest thrill was to be a part of the backstage production. Paul questioned why I didn't sit in the audience to enjoy the acts, so I explained that I was learning more by watching from behind the stage. To be alone with Australia's best comics as they prepared to step up was much more intriguing for me. I loved the fact that at one stage while Elliot was performing, Vince and Brad were engrossed in an NRL match on Vince's phone. Considering they both had performances to come, I was impressed by their confident and relaxed natures gained from decades of experience. However, every time Vince was about to step up as the headliner, I observed a regular pattern. With about five minutes to go, he would pace a little and go into his head. He didn't look nervous, just focused, like a rugby player about to run out for a big match. It reminded me of the zone I would often go into myself, where I had little recognition of anything the current act was saying as I was only focused on my own material. I felt a sense of validation, harking back to Station 59 nights when I'd roam the streets of Richmond, to observe that even the best comedians followed a similar practice. At times I wanted to ask Vince to what extent he felt nervous, but I didn't want to intrude upon his headspace, so I never asked. I'm sure that even though he knew his material backwards, he still viewed each gig as its own performance. Vince performs approximately 200 gigs per year, and I got the impression that every time he steps onto a stage, in front of a television audience of millions or a roomful of punters in Moorabin, he still wants to deliver his best performance to date. I was highly impressed. One night during this ritual, he paused to contemplate his shirt buttons and speculatively flicked open one more to reveal slightly more of his Italian chest hair and then glanced up at me, as if for approval. Understanding that this appearance related to his routine, I considered it and nodded affirmatively. He thanked me without words, and as he stepped up to another uproarious performance I basked in the glory that I had, in the smallest way possible, contributed to a performance by Australia's best comedian. Once again, I melted like plastic cheese on toast.

And I should point out at this stage that much of Vince's roof-raising material was the same as I remembered from *Hey Hey* three decades earlier. When I'd first met him at Blessington Street and tried to appeal to his sense of nostalgia by recalling my favourite memories of him, I had no idea that I was about to revisit many of them live on stage, including the cheese bit. I mean that with the highest praise, as the most endearing compliment a comedian can have is that their material stands up for such a long period of time. As Vince currently makes his living mostly from corporate gigs rather than television, his material is somewhat protected from repetition. But for him that wouldn't matter anyway, as his laughs are achieved equally through his animated persona. Even after four nights of witnessing the same routines, some I'd adored since my teenage years, I still laughed just as hard for the same reason that I can rewatch DVDs of Billy Connelly, Jim Jefferies and Adam Hills without getting sick of them. I was watching true comedic skill. No, comedic *art*.

When I discussed this with Paul, he grinned and said, 'Of course, mate. That's all it takes. If you've got an hour of absolutely solid, A+ material you can build a whole career around it.' Thinking about this blew my mind. And I noticed even

Elliot was using a lot of material from years ago, yet I was again laughing just as hard as I had as a teenager. To be clear, Vince and Elliot have both maintained fresh and innovative routines over their whole careers. But it was endearing to see their best material from the early days working just as well today.

After Friday's show, the second last of our run, we stayed back for late drinks after the bar had closed to punters and reflected upon the success of the shows to date. As I sat there enjoying a beer and a laugh around a table with my new mates Paul, his assistant Chantelle, Brad Oakes, Vince Sorrenti, Elliot Goblet, Nikki Osborne and her husband Jeremy, I had another of those pinch-yourself moments where I was so glad for the random series of events that had brought me here, made possible only by staying off my couch at times when it had been much more tempting to stay horizontal.

I was especially glad for this opportunity to relax and socialise tonight as I wasn't able to make our final show on Saturday. When I explained to Paul that it clashed with my father's bucks night, I'm sure at first he thought I was trying out new material. But Dad was getting remarried on the verge of his seventieth birthday, and I couldn't have been happier for him. I did not want to miss this dinner, even though I'm sure it wasn't going to be quite as lively as some bucks parties I'd experienced in my younger days. And while it would have been nice to see this production through to its conclusion, I was extremely content with my experience and the contribution I'd been able to make so far for St Kilda Comedy Club.

Chatting again with Nikki, who'd come to experience tonight's show in the venue we were sharing for our own shows next week, I sensed she was feeling just as nervous as I was. Apart from debuting at the festival, she still had the added stress of social media trolling that had not abated. I can't imagine how much that would have added to her anxiety, and I did my best to reassure both her and Paul that once people saw the show they would change their minds. I reminded Nikki that she had the best possible premise for a comedy festival show – her own personal narrative. She was telling a story only she could tell, and that made me want to hear it. I assured her that when people understood the celebratory nature of her show, the positive reviews would outweigh the vitriolic trolling. She thanked me, and I sensed my words might have made a difference. I hope they did, as I greatly admired her courage throughout the whole ordeal.

Above all else, I think the most rewarding part of this unique experience was getting to know Jack Levi. Throughout this story so far I've discussed meeting many people who are wonderfully genuine and positive (and mind you I've certainly met others who are not!), but of them all, I think Jack was a stand-out. Just like Vince and Brad, he is a celebrity without an air of pretension. And from the beginning, he took an avid interest in me and my journey. I've admired Elliot Goblet since I was a child, but from the first time I spoke to him I'd never felt a sense of being star-struck. He was an everyday bloke who recognised my efforts to break into the comedy scene. He asked me questions about my journey that no-one else ever bothered to. And every night as he appeared on the professional stage representing his own brand, he held aloft a copy of the *Herald Sun MICF Guide* and without obligation advertised *Tiff Upper Lip*.

'Ben Tiffen is an exciting new comedian who would be wonderful to watch,' he would promote in his ironically deadpan monotone. Again, my heart melted. I'd never been so overwhelmed by such an emotionless endorsement.

Appearing in the *Herald Sun* magazine was, to me, a defining moment. It was what I'd symbolically based my aspirations on. A sign of success, in some ways, and a thrill to appear alongside so many other, much more accomplished comedians in an equal format; apart from the paid advertising spaces that were larger on the page, every single act, big or small, was allotted equal advertising space in the general guide section. With acts listed alphabetically by first name, I was tucked in beside my new mate Bev Killick, and with a live-action picture of me performing at *The Brunny*, I did at least look the part of an accomplished comedian.

I was not fooling myself, however. Anyone who fronts the registration fee is entitled to the same advertising space. The MICF has no selection by merit, and for the first time it began to feel like less of an achievement and more of a self-imposed challenge. *Tiff Upper Lip* was to debut next week, and as I drove home I repeated my mantra ad nauseum: 'I'm not nervous, I'm excited.'

The next time I would be back here, there would be no Elliot, Vince or Brad. I would be the centre of attention for a full paying audience. I would be the show. I would be the reason why people were going out for the night, getting dressed up and organising babysitters. There was no way out now.

I had to deliver the goods.

18

THE BIG GIG

There is a little boy. He's in Grade Four, performing a series of solo comedy skits in front of his class at Montessori Primary School. *The Ben Tiffen Show*, he might have regretfully called it, but it was fun and he loved it. His comfort zone was much larger then.

Soon the boy is writing a movie script in Grade Six. It's for a *Star Wars* sequel that he is ambitiously hoping to make with some friends using his family's Super 8mm camera. One day his teacher catches him writing it in class when he's supposed to be doing maths and, fearing he'd get in trouble, he tries to hide it. However, when Mr Perry reads the script, he looks more intrigued than angry. Mr Perry challenges the boy to write a play in a similar style that could be produced by the class. The boy does so, and the comedic play becomes a rather obsessive project for Grade 6P, drawing upon elements of writing, acting, set and costume design, music and even electronics (one boy converted a remote control car into a dog). Many students agree it was one of their greatest experiences of primary school, and as the writer/director, the boy couldn't be happier. Later in life, as a teacher, he would be inspired by John Perry to favour hands-on experiences and give his own students every chance to explore their creativity to its fullest.

Now the boy is in Year Eight, competing in the drama category of the state-wide *Tournament of the Minds* with a parody of Shakespeare (*All the World's a Garbage Truck* was surprisingly deep for his age group). Frustratingly, his team finishes second overall, losing points because someone forgot to rewind the cassette with the music on it. The disappointing result somewhat clouds an otherwise fantastic experience, and the boy develops a distaste for competitive creativity. He believes art should just be enjoyed, not compared. Again in Year Eight, the boy is part of a group of five who recreate some of their funniest skits from drama class for the talent show on school camp. It brings tears of laughter from students and teachers alike. Among the group is a girl who was socially shunned and bullied by her peers. Children can be very cruel. This moment is perhaps the first time she embraces the experience of stepping up in front of a larger audience, and to witness the joy and acceptance she finally feels almost brings a tear to the boy's face as well. And all while still studying drama at the National Theatre. The boy truly loves having such a regular creative outlet.

But then nothing. Absolutely nothing for many years.

At Kingston City Hall, on the opening night of *Tiff Upper Lip*, I couldn't help but think of that boy as I quietly inspected the empty venue a couple of hours before the show. He would be so excited by this. My posters were displayed intermittently with Nikki Osborne's along the maroon carpet walkway from the main bar area to the ballroom, where Vince and Elliot had performed last week, giving both shows a sense of occasion that would have thrilled the boy no end. About seventy tickets had been sold for tonight, which was pleasing. Looking at the list of sales it was, as I'd expected, mostly friends and family, although importantly there were many coming who had never seen me perform, including Dad and his fiancé Maureen, my sister Kathy and her partner Hayden and my Aunty Jo. I was glad to finally provide them with a forum more conducive to a family night out.

Paul had set the ticket price to $21.80, and from the beginning I was concerned it was too high. I was aiming for $10, a token price that people are normally happy to punt with but not high enough to suggest my show was worth more than so many others in that range. However, I did understand that Paul was the producer and had expenses to pay, including the use of this venue and a technical assistant to operate my lights and music. He was spending money to produce a quality show for me, exactly what he'd promised, so I trusted him and wanted him to make a profit. I genuinely didn't care about profit for myself, as this was a life goal and my own profit was not relevant for now, but for Paul it was a business after all. And for the experiences he'd provided me so far, I owed his business more than just love. Besides, when Paul reminded me of how much work I'd put into my comedy to this point, including a workshop in New York, the price suddenly didn't seem so unreasonable. What the hell, I thought, I'd worked bloody hard to be in this position to give people a fun night out, what's wrong with asking for twenty bucks?

However, I still had one lingering concern. I have a long-held theory that as soon as a ticket price for anything exceeds $10, there is a part of the brain that stops enjoying the show in place of evaluating whether value for money is being obtained. And the higher the price, the more brain activity takes place. If a neurosurgeon was to hook up audience members to a brain scan, I'm sure the lobe that evaluates finances would be getting more and more luminous with every joke that doesn't get a belly laugh. It's only natural, I guess, but it was an important consideration. I wasn't stepping up at a free venue where nobody has a right to complain if an act bombs. I'd put myself on a platform where the commodity of laughter was now contractually required in exchange for a sum of money. Despite my confidence, it was still a daunting prospect.

It was reassuring to know, however, that my show was guaranteed some good early laughs. It's normal for such a show to employ an opening act, a strong comedian doing about ten minutes to not only give the audience extra value but, more importantly, to get them focused and laughing by the time the main act is introduced. It's an important role, similar to the one Brad played for Vince and Elliot, and I could only ask it of someone I trusted to do a superlative job. So I asked Mimi Shaheen. In the couple of years since her debut at Comedy Speed Dating, Mimi was excelling in the comedy scene and becoming widely recognised. She had the perfect style for welcoming an audience and getting big early laughs, and her inclusion gave my narrative a happily rounded feel (when I told the story of Comedy Speed Dating, the audience was delighted to hear it's where Mimi had started – the greatest love she found through my dating business was one for the stage). When I asked Mimi whether she'd do this for me I was worried she'd be too busy working with more accomplished comedians. She was part of a festival show called *Did we just become best friends?* But I couldn't have been more wrong. She was honoured to accept the role and thanked me wholeheartedly. She gladly agreed to do four of my five shows, as she was occupied with her own show for the other night, and excitedly shared social media posts to promote *Tiff Upper Lip*. She felt anxious about doing a good job for me, but I reassured her that I knew she would be perfect; my only concern was that the audience would be talking about her act instead of mine!

Standing on the stage I now looked out across the ballroom – empty but for the round tables and the technician checking the lights and audio. I gave him a couple of sound checks, and then couldn't resist taking a selfie, mic in hand and the ballroom my background, to post on Facebook, noting, 'Only a couple of hours until show time!' It got an excited response, particularly from those getting ready to come in. But the most excited person was undoubtedly me.

And so was the little boy who loved to perform. He was beaming that *The Ben Tiffen Show* had finally made it onto a bigger stage.

Waiting backstage with Mimi, I was pacing the same floor I'd watched Vince Sorrenti pace a week earlier. It felt bare without the others here, especially Paul who had to prioritise Nikki's debut, a one-off show at St Kilda Sports Club. Tomorrow she would be joining me here as the second part of our double act. I was very grateful for Mimi's company tonight.

'You'll be great,' she said, sensing my nerves.

'Let's hope so,' I replied. Overall, I was happy with the way my show had developed. I think I'd structured it well, with the first half focusing on the importance of keeping a stiff upper lip through life's adversities, incorporating old and new material, and the second half focusing on my dating adventures and starting a speed dating business – effectively a reworking of my Fringe show. Between the two halves I'd also planned a 'talk to the audience' section. Generally, I was feeling good that I now had a much better idea of who I was on the stage, and I was telling a story that only I could tell. A year or so ago, I could make neither of those claims.

Still, I was feeling naturally anxious, especially as the ballroom on the other side of the curtain began to fill with the familiar hum of voices. And this time, the voices were more familiar than ever, as I recognised a random assortment of friends, family and work colleagues. I did my best to keep channelling this into excitement. This was what I'd been building up towards these past six months, or realistically much longer. This was why my name and picture was in the *Herald Sun* magazine and my poster was displayed at the Melbourne Town Hall. This was the pinnacle of my journey to date, and if it didn't go well it would be extremely disappointing.

On cue, the house lights faded and the catchy opening riffs of *Stiff Upper Lip* rang out across the room. Brian Johnson of AC/DC delivered the first words of my show, as he belted out a fitting introduction:

'Well I was out on a drive, on a bit of a trip
Lookin' for thrills, to get me some kicks
Now, I warn you ladies, I shoot from the hip
I was born with a stiff, stiff upper lip.'

Backstage, in my ringside announcer voice, I welcomed the audience to Kingston City Hall and introduced Mimi on stage.

Mimi absolutely smashed it. I couldn't have been happier with her ten minutes. The crowd was warmed up and settling into a night of laughter. But then I made a small mistake. I had asked Mimi to do her ten minutes and then announce a five-minute break to refresh drinks, before I would come out as the main act. This was for the audience's convenience, as the bar was a fair walk away and I wanted to give people a chance to stock up on drinks for my set, but it was also because I didn't want people walking in and out while I was performing. It made good sense at the time, however I think the break stifled the great momentum Mimi had created for my entrance. It was a simple mistake, nothing too bad, but one that I rectified for the following shows.

As we'd already used *Stiff Upper Lip*, I chose to walk out after the break to *Welcome to the Jungle* by Guns n' Roses – a rock star entrance that probably satisfied other fantasies along the way – and ripped into my longest and most important comedy set to date.

I think my show started pretty well. I didn't forget any early material, a major relief, and heard good laughter in the right places. Unfortunately, I could no longer use the very strong Pauline Hanson bit as its shelf-life was over – the downside of jokes based on current events – so I replaced it with one about the Australian cricket team and the recent ball tampering controversy. It wasn't quite as strong, but it got a good laugh and tied in nicely with my theme of keeping a stiff upper lip through adversity. Thankfully, I relaxed into my performance early, and began enjoying myself. Perhaps my biggest challenge was the physical distance between myself and the audience. It wasn't huge, but they certainly felt farther away than I was used to. I struggled a bit during the section devoted to talking to the audience, relying on a bit of practised spontaneity, but I gave up pretty early as there was only one table I could actually see through the lights, and they were shy to converse. I punctuated the end of the first section with a cheap gag I'd thought of at the last minute, which was to become one of my most enduring bits. I explained that it's hard for comedians to make much money these days, so I was selling a DVD for just $10. Of course, it's not unusual for comedians to sell merchandise after their shows (a week ago I'd strived to sell Goblet socks), so it came across as an early plug, until I held aloft a DVD of *Gladiator* with Russell Crowe, and explained, 'I don't want this one anymore…'. As I progressed on the circuit, it became a regular gag of mine to use a different movie selection each week and joke about why I needed to get rid of it.

The second half of the show was even more enjoyable for me, as I had momentum by now, and lately I'd had the most fun telling narratives. I added a couple of new bits, but it was pretty much the same story as from my Fringe show, concluding with an unveiling of my Comedy Speed Dating banner to victorious applause. And it perfectly accentuated my message of keeping a stiff upper lip. I felt it had been an uplifting one that held my show together coherently and left the audience feeling positive. While I had no 'Touch the frog' gospel-style ending, I hope I had at least inspired people to stay positive and touch their frogs in whatever context that may be. Later that night I was to go home and touch my own frog, the Year Eight drama award (the 'Kermit') won by the boy who loved to perform, and I felt a reconnection with him like never before.

By the time I got off stage to what felt like great applause, Mimi greeted me backstage and told me gushingly that she'd loved it. I thanked her wholeheartedly for her hilarious contribution which had made the evening work. Then I took a moment to simply breathe out. Straight after my first performance at Station 59, more than four years ago, was perhaps the last time I'd felt such a surge of relief. Back then

I'd fulfilled a life goal just by finding the courage to attempt stand up comedy in the corner of a Richmond pub and push through some failed punchlines. Now I'd performed at the Melbourne International Comedy Festival. I let that sink in for a moment.

For me this had been a great personal success but, self-consciously, I was still concerned about how well the audience had enjoyed it and whether they felt satisfied. Many would have no concept of the arduous journey I'd been through to get here – they were just analysing whether it had been worth twenty bucks. Which is showbiz, no doubt. They seemed to have laughed well in the right places, but instinctively I felt it had not surpassed my Friday night Fringe show, which I'll always remember as my most fun gig to date. Perhaps this could be attributed to the less intimate venue, the fact it was now ticketed, or simply that several people here tonight had been to Highlander and had heard much of this routine before. There are many factors that contribute to a successful comedy show that can go well beyond the quality of material and its delivery. I guess there was only one way left to get an additional sense of feedback. It was the part of the night I was looking forward to the most – socialising with my audience in the bar. I think in a small-scale production such as mine it's important to interact with as many people as you can after the show, to thank them for coming and hopefully extend their enjoyment of the evening beyond the performance itself.

As the audience was mostly people I knew, many of them gave me a hug, congratulating me and letting me know how much they'd enjoyed the show. Mostly obligatory praise, I understood, and it was hard to tell how sincere people were being, but I basked in all accolades anyway.

There were two pieces of feedback I appreciated the most. The first was from Carol, a former English teacher at my school, who sought me out through the crowd to thank me. Presently in retirement, she explained she'd seen several other, more well-known comedians throughout the festival, and my show had made her laugh more than theirs. I could tell she was sincere, and that meant a lot to me. The other was from Andrew, who had been there with his wife Alison when I'd made my laugh-less debut at Station 59. They'd both attended tonight with their son Ben, and were two of the very few people to understand my full journey. With a broad smile, Andrew shook my hand firmly and said, 'That was great, mate, that was really funny. I mean that.' We shared a couple of laughs over bits such as my generally unsuccessful attempts to meet women in nightclubs (which he'd related to because he was normally beside me at the time). This was my favourite endorsement of all because, having known Andrew for many years, I knew him to be the sort of bloke who would never say such a thing unless he truly meant it. He wouldn't tell me immediately after the show if he didn't like it, he'd most likely wait a while and find something else to praise for now ('It took a lot of guts to get up there,' was feedback I'd heard before from several people). This was his first genuine praise of my material and craft, and I took it to heart.

I couldn't find my family after the show, but that was ok. Kathy texted me to say that Dad was a bit emotional, thankfully for good reasons. He knew how much I used to love drama and how much work I'd put into this new endeavour. He has always been very supportive of anything I wanted to try and he recognised how much this had meant to me. I was happy that at this age I could still try new things to make him proud. Also,

Kathy said they had all been very touched by the shout out I'd given them at the end of my show.

'And finally… is there a Ron and Maureen in the house?' I had said. After a short pause came a familiar voice.

'I'm a Ron!'

'Folks, a little birdie tells me that Ron and Maureen are getting married in a couple of weeks, so I'd like to wish the newlyweds all the best for their wedding!'

This received warm applause, happily embarrassing them a little. Then I made a reference to an earlier bit about the difficulty of finding a rhyming pun for Tiffen, explaining 'Ron would know because he's also a Tiffen. This is my father. Dad and Maureen. Love you guys, all the very best.'

As you know, I am not a religious man, nor one to believe in fate, but I've always felt the timing of my debut show landing days before my father's second wedding to be at least fortuitous. To have a public forum in which to express my love for my father before such a major event gave my festival show an additional sense of meaning.

The following night I was feeling slightly less anxious, but with a whole new audience of roughly the same number – plus Paul for the first time, and Nikki who was performing on the same stage after my show – I felt the customary butterflies headbutting my stomach as show time approached. Fortunately, I was again confident of early laughs through my opening act. On this occasion it wasn't Mimi, as tonight was the night our shows clashed, so I'd employed the service of another key figure of my story – Mr Evan Hocking. Paul was thrilled that I was able to draw such a well-known identity to open my show, and

I was grateful for an opportunity to involve him. Again, my only worry was that he'd be funnier than me.

Before the show, Evan and I were hanging out backstage chatting about recent gigs, and he was fascinated to hear of my experiences with Vince and Elliot. Then he excused himself and ducked out, leaving me a window to revise my material. I appreciated the warm-up time, but as the familiar hum of a filling audience began to increase, I glanced at my watch to realise it was only a few minutes until the intro music would start, and Evan wasn't back yet. As I had no direct communication with the technician who was about to play the music, and Paul was occupied with loading the audience, I began to panic. If the show began without Evan I wouldn't know what to do, and I had no idea where he was. Then I noticed a message on my phone: 'Just on the shitter mate I'm 2 mins away'. Oh great, I thought. But at least I could now focus on my opening lines again. He promptly returned and gave me a good pump-up like a footy coach, which helped. To the opening riffs of *Stiff Upper Lip*, I announced him on stage and he bounded up the stairs and got good laughs from the beginning.

As much fun as comedy is, the ten minutes before going on stage was still for me the most excruciating time of any gig. Listening to Evan, I got a buzz from every big laugh he was extracting from our audience. However, in my nervous state, I also began thinking about something entirely different. Evan's text had reminded me that I hadn't been to the toilet before the show. In fact, in what might have been a bit of overconfidence, I'd had a full chicken parma about ninety minutes ago and washed it down with a couple of pints of beer, and now I was feeling an increasing need to evacuate it. Alarm bells blared in my mind. Perhaps Evan's poo had been a professional one.

Was this another reminder of my amateur status? The more I thought about this, the more I began to feel certain muscles working harder against my natural gait.

As Evan continued getting laughs, I felt my situation becoming more dire. The mind is a powerful tool, and the more I considered the potential of having a poo right now the more my bowels agreed it would be a good idea to do so. Suddenly I cursed myself for cancelling the break between acts, as I couldn't see myself holding out for almost an hour. I estimated there were approximately six minutes before he announced me on stage and realised I had only two options. Firstly, I could run through the ballroom, have a four minute poo, and run back again in time to go on stage. Alternatively, I could risk shitting my pants on stage in front of my entire paying audience. Bizarrely, I took a punt on the latter.

As he called me on stage, I waddled up the stairs like an excited duck and burst into my routine. Fortunately, as soon as my mind was on the task of entertaining I somehow forgot about my more immediate concern and managed to survive the show without a graphic interlude. It would surely have been the most awkward issuing of a refund in the history of the MICF. To stand out among 600 acts was difficult, but this was not the way I wanted to make the papers. So I was proud of myself on more than one level. Straight after the gig I was into the toilets before the outro music had finished. It's a mark of a good show when audience members hold onto their toilet needs until the end, and I was quietly impressed not only that nobody had snuck out early, but that I had beaten everyone else to the loo.

It reiterated to me once again just how many things good comedians need to think about before and during any show.

These are some of the most talented and professional performers in the entire world.

I truly, truly believe that.

I think my second show went as well as opening night. I was pretty happy with it, and Paul and Nikki were delighted. My great mate Matty Fergo filmed parts of it from the front table, but to this day I still haven't watched it back. I'm not exactly sure why – perhaps it's because the show sits well in my memory, and if I watch it I will probably be hypercritical of myself. I stayed to watch Nikki's show which went very well too, and I assisted by filming. While I liked the show, Nikki wasn't completely happy with it. Backstage, she expressed concern over a couple of flat spots. Overall, I thought it had worked well as a humorous narrative. The critics had been wrong to suggest the show would be in bad taste, as it was more a celebration of her son's autism than a parody and it worked towards breaking down prejudices. Nevertheless, with the assistance of Bev Killick she rewrote some sections, and when I saw the show again the following week it was even funnier.

I could now relax for the first time in a while. My next shows were a few days away, on Wednesday, Thursday and Friday, and to be honest I would have been happy for my festival run to end tonight while I was on a high. By now I could feel satisfied without the stress of three more shows, which were shaping up to be more challenging. Ticket sales were relatively low and, as a result, Kingston City Hall had scheduled them for the bar area. I've seen plenty of great festival shows in bars, but they'd been in 'proper' bars, not the relatively sterile environment of a council building, which I felt would lack atmosphere and a sense of occasion. Despite this, I told myself I could embrace it as a valuable test of my endurance and adaptability – essential qualities for comedians. I was going to find out what kind of steel I was made of.

As it turned out, the less said about the bar shows probably the better. The audiences were very small on Wednesday and Thursday and the cavernous space didn't work well, with most audience members choosing to sit towards the rear of the bar despite Mimi's attempts to coax them forward. I'd seen Evan successfully entertain a small crowd, but now I understood why he'd used a much smaller, more intimate room. My final show on Friday was better, attracting a few more good friends unwinding at the end of the week, but ultimately I wish I'd been able to funnel my audiences into just the two ballroom shows. I'm sure a more accomplished comedian could have made the bar shows work well, so I couldn't fully blame the venue. I'd put myself in a position where crowd work was more important than ever without yet mastering the skill. Overall, I was delighted with *Tiff Upper Lip*, but the lessons kept coming, and it reinforced to me how skilful the best comedians actually are.

Since then, I've wondered at times whether I went too early with my festival show. Could I have produced a better show with an extra year or two of experience? To be honest, of course I could have. But I'm sure the same can be said of any show. Obviously, with hindsight I would have done some things differently. It was Steven Wright who said 'Experience is something you don't get until just after you need it.' And I'm fully aware that my journey to becoming proficient at this exceedingly complex artform is still very much in its infancy. But *Tiff Upper Lip* was a story that could only have been told at this time. To be true to what I'd learned, if I'd waited longer, the story of Comedy Speed Dating would not have been as relevant to me and my performance would have lacked emotional fullness. Since then I think I've written better material and developed my stage persona much further. I've become more clean-cut as I've been crystalising who I am on the stage. But throughout the entire journey, I'd been an advocate for embracing challenges and not procrastinating, as you never know what opportunities may present themselves, nor which obstacles may appear. For example, it may sound far-fetched, but imagine if a global pandemic struck, heavily impacting the amateur comedy scene for at least two years and resulting in entire festivals being cancelled. As ridiculous as that may sound, you just never, ever know what may be around the corner if you wait too long.

For almost four years I was blessed to have Sarah by my side through so many of my pivotal moments. Our lives crossing at this point made it possible for this story to unfold, and we'll share many memories of fun times that would have seemed so unlikely before meeting. Sadly, we parted ways in 2018, our lives simply taking us in different directions, parting amicably and hopefully remaining friends. It reminded me that life doesn't follow a script. As human beings we innately want it to. But perhaps life is really just a bunch of stuff that happens, and comedy is one way we make sense of it all.

I will always cherish our fun times, and I'm sure the next phase of my life will be as memorable in its own right.

A question I hear a lot is 'Why do you do it?'. It's one I've often contemplated. I understand it's normally asked in the context of 'Why do you put yourself through so much stress and potential humiliation just to tell a few jokes?', which for many would sound completely insane, especially for those who fear and loathe public speaking. But to be honest, I think for me the best answer is the simplest. I do it because I enjoy it. I enjoy the challenge of both writing and performing. I enjoy the social life. I normally enjoy the nights of comedy and the thousands of acts I've watched. I particularly enjoy the exhilaration of riding a big wave of laughter. I have truly enjoyed reconnecting with my younger self and discovering a new creative outlet (I strongly believe everyone should have a creative outlet in whatever form that appeals to them). And I've enjoyed learning a lot about myself, stepping out of my comfort zone as inspired to do so by my own students way back in 2013. Overall, why wouldn't we spend our time doing things we enjoy? I'm guessing nobody ever got to the end of their life and regretted not spending more time on the couch.

After my second night in the ballroom at Kingston City Hall, I was thrilled that a lot of my friends were still hanging around, socialising in the bar. In a distinct moment of reflection, I stood back and enjoyed the scene. Laughs were flowing freely, and for the second night in a row, mates from different areas of my life were bonding and having a great time. Evan was still here as well, enjoying a beer with the people he'd just met. My comedy show had brought strangers together and set the tone for the night. And I'd been a part of so many other fun times through comedy – great evenings of laughter with friends old or new, fond memories to share with Matthew, eclectic date nights, and fun nights when I'd gone out alone, whether here or on the other side of the globe. In a world where the nightly news is often depressing, and even downtime can be taken way too seriously (I don't need to hear about another 'crisis' at a football club), it's a relief to stop and see the funny side of life in the limited time we have on this earth. How hard can it truly be?

So as I continued relaxing and enjoying the company of friends who, like me, would most likely otherwise be at home selecting between the hundreds of options we now have on TV – and maybe choosing between the dozens of home food delivery services available in a world where it could be argued we are being manipulated to spend even less time going outside – I considered perhaps this was the reason why I do it. If there was a greater purpose to comedy, it might be driven by nothing more than a yearning to get out, get together, enjoy human connection and one of the most basic desires of all – to laugh together and share a humorous perspective on the world, and ourselves.

After all, we can all use a bit of a laugh.

ABOUT THE AUTHOR

Ben Tiffen has been a secondary English teacher since 2005, and of all the challenges in teaching English, the one he most enjoys is helping young people to tell their own story and find their own voice. He delights in watching his students' literacy and self-confidence grow, and strongly believes that everyone has an interesting story to tell. There was never any doubt that Ben would one day write a memoir himself.

Born in Melbourne in 1973, Ben grew up loving drama, reading, writing, stand-up comedy and Aussie Rules football. He attended the first Montessori primary school in Victoria and developed a keen interest in creative arts, and later educational theory. He also attended Melbourne High School, however he didn't finish there, as when his family moved from Elsternwick to Mount Waverley, he wanted to change schools to meet new, local friends. To this day he remains the only student in history to transfer from Melbourne High to Syndal Tech. It was a move he has never regretted.

Today, Ben most enjoys spending quality time with his family and friends. He likes traveling to exciting destinations when time, money and pandemics allow for it, and he continues to perform stand-up. This is his first book.

www.ingramcontent.com/pod-product-compliance
Lightning Source LLC
LaVergne TN
LVHW051825080426
835512LV00018B/2733